RADICAL ALIGNMENT

The Surprising Journey of
Becoming an Intentional Church

RADICAL ALIGNMENT

The Surprising Journey of Becoming an Intentional Church

BART RENDEL AND DOUG PARKS

IntentionalChurches.com

Radical Alignment: The Surprising Journey of Becoming an Intentional Church
Copyright © 2025 by Intentional Churches®

Written by Bart Rendel and Doug Parks
Cofounders, Intentional Churches

Published by IC Press, a division of Intentional Churches®
840 S. Rancho Dr. #4-414
Las Vegas, NV 89106

All rights reserved. Except for brief excerpts for review purposes, no part of this publication may be reproduced or used in any form without the prior permission of the publisher, except as provided by USA copyright law.

All Scripture quotations are taken from the Holy Bible, New Living Translation, copyright © 1996, 2004, 2015 by Tyndale House Foundation. Used by permission of Tyndale House Publishers, Inc., Carol Stream, Illinois 60188. All rights reserved.

ISBN (paperback) 979-8-9998582-0-7
ISBN (ePub) 979-8-9998582-2-1

Intentional Churches®, ChurchOS®, Engagement Pathway®, Great Commission Engine®, Intentional Growth Planning®, Living Toolbox®, Activation Dashboard™, IGP™, Priorities for Impact™, Relational Reach Zone™, Six Domains of Impact™, The Radical Alignment Assessment™, The Radical Alignment Index™, The Radical Alignment Dashboard™, OneTeam™, OneBoard™, OneLife™, Vision Initiative Project™, One-Aware Filter™, and One-Aware Weekend™ are trademarks of Intentional Churches.

Four Helpful Lists is used by permission of Paterson Center, LLC.

Cover and Interior Design: Ember Brand Co.

Printed in the United States of America

**Dedicated to the leaders of
Intentional Churches everywhere**

CONTENTS

Introduction
Well, Hello There! ix

Chapter 1
1,000 Churches (and Counting) 1

Chapter 2
5 Challenging Discoveries 13

Chapter 3
5 Encouraging Discoveries 35

Chapter 4
One Solution 55

Chapter 5
7 Steps to Jump-Start the Journey 81

Chapter 6
3 Ways to Not Get Stuck 109

Foundations
25 Foundational Beliefs 125

INTRODUCTION

Well, Hello There!

Well, hello there!

You might be wondering, Who are you guys? And, What is Intentional Churches?

Intentional Churches is kind of hard to describe. For starters, it's a ministry organization based in Las Vegas, Nevada, with staff and coaches spread around the country. We don't really have formal offices, and most of our meetings occur on Zoom, in a home, in a church, or at a coffee shop.

Intentional Churches is also a community of churches and leaders who have committed to collaborating with each other to reach more people for Christ. We sometimes use the word *movement* to describe this community, and in this book, you are going to learn more about what makes it a movement.

We'll tell you right up front—we hope you jump in with both feet. But we also know that's not how it really works. We need to get to know each other first.

We (Doug and Bart) are both husbands, fathers, church leaders, and passionate followers of Jesus Christ. We felt the call of God on both our lives to serve in the local church as pastors and then the church at large by starting Intentional Churches. We have thirty-five combined years in previous vocational ministry as executive leaders, serving on the teams of both church plants and large established churches.

Sometimes, we get asked what it feels like no longer being in local church ministry. The funny thing is, we both feel just as connected to church leadership, if not more so, than ever before. Church leaders and leadership are our passion. We will both be living out this passion for the rest of our lives.

We started Intentional Churches about a dozen years ago. We created the Intentional Churches Toolbox and wrote a book about it titled *Intentional Churches: How Implementing an Operating System Clarifies Vision, Improves Decision Making, and Stimulates Growth*. We'll tell you more about that and what we've learned by helping churches and leaders align with the Great Commission.

Our staff and coaching team have seen it all, but we don't really consider ourselves to be consultants or church doctors. We are more like personal trainers who've created an adaptable leadership system for any church that wants to reach more people and grow them in Christ. Over the years, we've grown into a community of leaders learning together every day what it means to lead an Intentional Church.

We are just stewards of the growing movement.

This book was written for the leaders of Intentional Churches everywhere—elders, pastors, staff, and lay leaders—because radical alignment begins with you. Church leadership is one of the highest and hardest callings anyone can follow. You are special to us, and it's no small thing that you've chosen to join us by engaging the ideas in this book.

Thank you to our Activator and coaching communities for your inspiration, encouragement, and belief in Intentional Churches. Thanks to Scott Watson for your insights, exposition, and tying all of this to a powerful assessment. Assessing the truth of our circumstances and scriptural reflection is always the place to start. Thanks to Krista Dunbar for capturing stories of churches on the surprising journey of becoming an Intentional Church. And finally, thanks to the Berg Family Foundation for caring about radical alignment to the Great Commission as much as we do.

That's enough for now. Let's go!

For Individual Reflection and Application:

1. Where is your passion for ministry right now? Where was it when you got into ministry? What were/are the key factors in seasons of excitement and momentum?

2. Do you have a community of leaders around you? What are the costs of not having one, and what are/would be the benefits?

For Team Discussion and Interaction:

1. Have you served on a team where there was a leadership model in place that unified the team's approach to ministry? If so, share what that looked like. If not, discuss what you think the benefits of one would be.

2. Are you ready to begin with honest assessment? Set the stage by sharing any reticence you have in beginning with an assessment of your current situation driven by scriptural reflection.

CHAPTER 1

1,000 Churches (and Counting)

Radical alignment is not our idea. It's been God's idea since the beginning. All of Scripture, the arc of the entire story, is a call to radically align with Him.

Think about it. From the warnings in the garden, to the law that condemned us, to the cross that reconciled us, to the Great Commission that sends us, to the letters to the seven churches in Revelation that warn us—God has always been about radical alignment to His good and perfect will.

This is true in both life and church leadership. You, your team, and your church have been called to fully align to His purposes.

> **God has always been about radical alignment to His good and perfect will.**

Have you thought of church leadership this way? It's true, but we don't want you to just take our word for it. We believe it's the testimony of Scripture again and again. We want to show you and help you begin the surprising journey of becoming an Intentional Church.

In Revelation 3, there is a phrase repeated to the seven churches: "Anyone with ears to hear must listen to the Spirit and understand what he is saying to the churches" (v. 6). The journey starts with listening, and by listening, conviction and action follow.

We've been doing a lot of listening and assessment over the past dozen years. We have worked directly with more than 1,000 churches that span the gamut of the church universe.

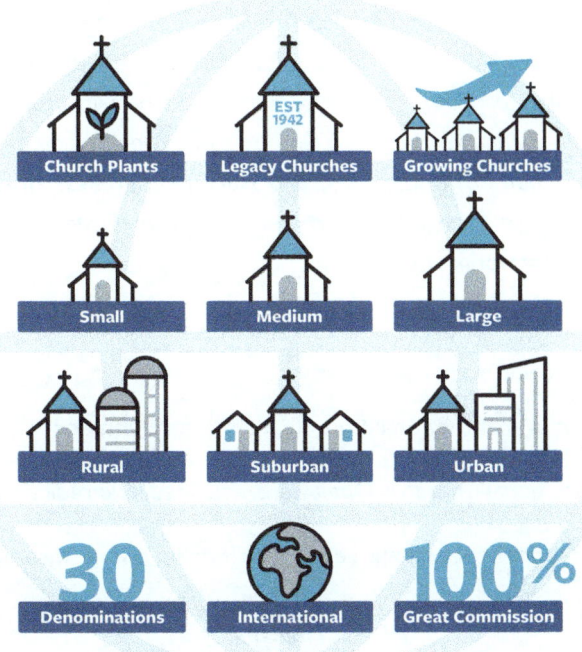

We've learned some things in all this work. What works. What doesn't. And why some churches succeed in creating lasting alignment while others fail to align to God's mission for their church.

We have carried the same intentions we established years ago throughout all of this work. We are more clear, convicted, and confident than ever in our mission and vision.

The Mission. *Intentional Churches exists to inspire, equip, and activate a movement of evangelistically effective churches that endure for generations.*

The Vision. *Intentional Churches' vision is to see thousands of churches collaborating to reach millions for Christ, who in turn reach millions more. As a basis for collaboration, these churches use similar teaching, tools, and methods to remain grounded and radically aligned to the Great Commission. They prevail by training leaders, multiplying disciples, and starting churches. Finally, they become experts in innovation and change management, creating generational longevity.*

THE INTENTIONAL CHURCH

So, what is an Intentional Church? Here's our definition:

The Intentional Church is *One-aware, activated, and radically aligned.*

But what does that mean? Let's break it down phrase by phrase.

The One
A reference to the lost sheep from Luke 15.

Aware
Having knowledge or perception of a situation or fact, concerned and well-informed.

Activated
Making something active or operative.

Radical
Affecting the fundamental nature of something, far-reaching and thorough.

Alignment
A position of agreement and alliance.

Now, let's put it all together into a simple description of the Intentional Church:

> The Intentional Church is concerned and well-informed about the lost, proactively keeping them top of mind. This knowledge and way of operating is so fundamental, far-reaching, and thorough that it becomes a key source of agreement and alliance in the church.

That sounds like an Intentional Church, doesn't it? One against which the gates of hell will not prevail.

Does that sound like your church? We hope so! And if not, we're going to show you how to get there. If you're already there, there's work to do to stay that way.

One church, on one mission. For generations.

Here are some characteristics of the Intentional Church.

- *The Intentional Church* resists the standard (and flawed) belief that there is a mandatory life cycle to the existence of a church. It has its ups and downs as all churches do, but it's built to last and remains God's primary plan to redeem the world.

- *The Intentional Church* is a learning organization. It is adaptive—a place where change becomes normal. The message stays consistent, but the methods are always on the table. One-awareness and activation require it!

- *The Intentional Church* grows naturally in depth and breadth. It adds to its number daily (because of an activated Ninety-Nine, the term we use for the flock from Luke 15) and enjoys the "favor of all the people" like the early church.

- *The Intentional Church* challenges every believer to make the Great Commission a personal mission statement in life and leadership. It proactively seeks to create radical alignment of the board, leadership team, and congregation.

UNDERWAY

It's happening. The movement of Intentional Churches is underway.

What can you learn from 1,000 churches? A lot!

But you know how it goes. As you mature and gain more knowledge, you also realize you don't know all that much yet. You gain valuable perspective. You learn where you are gifted, where your strengths lie, and the lane in which you were designed to run. You also learn where your weaknesses are and how to adjust and make improvements. You spot the gaps and try to close them.

That's how it's been for us.

We've made discoveries, adjusted course, and adapted along the way. We've had to fight for alignment ourselves, personally and as a ministry, and learn what it takes to maintain it. Most importantly, God continues to give us insight into what the stewardship of this movement will really require. We'll be sharing those discoveries and insights on the pages that follow.

This book will serve as a prequel of sorts to our *Intentional Churches* book—the kind you write when you start something, pause for a minute, and look back. The look-back is something we teach churches to do. It's a critical practice in staying aligned to the mission. You can learn so much, spot trends internally and externally, find plenty to celebrate, and ultimately gain wisdom for the road ahead.

We have a few goals. First, we want to share lessons learned the hard way from the trenches of ministry in the local church. That experience taught us a lot about radical alignment. We also want to share the biblical and convicting basis for the call to be radically aligned to the Great Commission and God's will for the church. And, perhaps most importantly, we want to equip you, your team, and your church to be radically aligned for the sake of the gospel.

We will:

- Share our discoveries.
- Reveal a new (old) solution.
- Reinforce key principles of alignment.
- Envision the future of a radically aligned church.
- Kick-start the alignment journey.
- Equip you to make progress.
- Give you some questions to consider.
- Set you up for collaboration.

In the end, we hope this book will inspire and challenge you to do what it takes to be an Intentional Church—a One-aware, activated, and radically aligned church.

AWAKENING

We are in a spiritual awakening. God is on the move, opening the hearts of Ones all around us. Young families who haven't been to church recently, if at all, are showing up. Revival is breaking out on college campuses across America. Bible sales are booming. You can sense the yearning in our culture and around the world for something different, for a new foundation and course for life.

Simply put, people are looking for hope, healing, and direction—the kind only Jesus can deliver.

The world has always needed One-aware, activated, and radically aligned churches. But today's awakening makes that truth all the more poignant. The time is *now* to dig in and do what it takes to become an Intentional Church. Let's shamelessly take advantage of this season of ministry.

Let's also commit to being fundamentally different on the other side of it. It's one thing to experience the fresh wind of the Spirit's influence and enjoy the fruit of it in our churches. It's another to commit to the transformation required, personally and organizationally, to be radically aligned to the Great Commission *permanently*.

Radical alignment will come easily to some of you. For others, it will take a lot of time, effort, and patience. Regardless of which scenario applies to you, we know you need the conviction, tools, and relationships to get there and stay there.

The more we study the lessons learned and examine the alignment arc in Scripture, the more deeply convicted and concerned we become about the state of church leadership today. At the same time, we become more inspired to help you and your church radically align to the cause of Christ in the world.

Let's start with some of our most pertinent discoveries from the past dozen years of working with 1,000 churches.

For Individual Reflection and Application:

1. How would you honestly assess your church against the definition of an Intentional Church: "One-aware, activated, and radically aligned"? Where are your strengths, weaknesses, or gaps?

2. Consider the characteristics of an Intentional Church listed in this chapter. Which one challenges you most personally, and why?

3. Reflect on your personal journey as a church leader. Where do you see God's hand in bringing you to this point of considering radical alignment?

For Team Discussion and Interaction:

1. What hopes and concerns do you have as you begin or continue this journey toward becoming an Intentional Church?

2. Is your church experiencing a spiritual renewal or revival? If so, share some stories as examples. If not, what will it take to participate in the current spiritual awakening? What must fundamentally and permanently change?

AN INTENTIONAL CHURCH STORY

From Obstacles to Opportunities: How Radical Alignment is Transforming Shelter Cove's Kingdom Impact

When Shelter Cove Community Church in Modesto, California, committed to radical alignment with the Great Commission, they experienced something extraordinary: they achieved their goal of doubling kingdom impact in just three years instead of four. But with explosive growth came new challenges that required creative solutions and unwavering trust in God's plan.

Lead Pastor Jeremy Oldenburger and Executive Pastor Jeremy Thiessen (JT) discovered that radical alignment meant more than just growing attendance—it required fundamentally rethinking how they approached ministry. When JT initially questioned why so many church transfers were coming instead of the "lost," their Small Groups Director offered a kingdom perspective: God was sending mature believers who could immediately lead and disciple the unchurched people still to come. One such leader now hosts small groups five nights a week, demonstrating how God orchestrates growth beyond human planning.

The transformation went deeper than strategy—it required a new vision rooted in Scripture's unchanging truth: "So that everyone would know him." This eternal vision replaced seasonal goals and became the driving force behind every decision.

Perhaps most significantly, Shelter Cove shifted from "come and see" to "go and tell" methodology. Their massive fall festival that drew 6,000 people resulted in only 2-3 new families—a sobering return on investment. In response, they created "One Night" on Halloween, encouraging members to engage neighbors in their own front yards instead of bringing them to church property.

To keep the mission visual and tangible, they created a giant number "1" filled with green ping-pong balls representing people being prayed for, and a cross filled with red balls celebrating salvations. One powerful Saturday night, a woman placed her friend's name on a green ball, watched him accept Christ during service, saw him get baptized spontaneously, then moved his name to a red ball in the cross—a perfect picture of the Great Commission in action.

Shelter Cove's journey proves that when churches radically align every strategy, resource, and event with reaching the One, God multiplies impact beyond imagination. Their story challenges pastors everywhere: What would happen if your entire ministry was filtered through the lens of the Great Commission?

Read Shelter Cove's Full Story Here

CHAPTER 2

5 Challenging Discoveries

Intentional Churches is a community of leaders who are committed to learning and advancing together. As a part of our training, we teach teams how to use a cycle called Intentional Growth Planning. It is a simple process that helps you get and stay aligned, and it includes seasons of reflection. God teaches us things we'd otherwise miss if we didn't pause and look back.

We are going to reflect and share some challenging discoveries along with our learnings. These discoveries represent headwinds to our ministry and the Intentional Churches movement. There are forces challenging our (and potentially your) progress.

This book is meant to be practical, so maybe you can identify with our observations and grab a few actionable observations as we go along.

CHALLENGING DISCOVERY #1:
This Is Going to Be Harder than We Thought

When we started Intentional Churches, we had a big vision and high hopes. We gathered our friends to speak into the launch and provide direction. Our vision was to see thousands of churches collaborating to reach millions for Christ. Today, more than ever, that vision compels and guides us. We knew it would take a common approach to ministry, lots of collaboration, and tenacity to see it through.

We identified the first phase as getting 1,000 churches to join the movement, which we knew would require meeting with churches one by one. We gave ourselves five years to make phase one happen, prayed it would only take three, and off we went—meeting, learning, codifying, teaching, and training.

As they say, ignorance is bliss. We are a dozen years in, and with hindsight, we had no idea how difficult it would be to accomplish phase one, let alone achieve the ultimate vision.

But why has it been so challenging?

Reason #1:
Our enemy doesn't want any of this to succeed.

We're stating the obvious.

> *For we are not fighting against flesh-and-blood enemies, but against evil rulers and authorities of the unseen world, against mighty powers in this dark world, and against evil spirits in the heavenly places.*
> —Ephesians 6:12

Again, in Thessalonians, it's clear that the progress of the Gospel is hindered by the work of Satan. Or, read the book of Acts to spot a few instances!

Things haven't changed all that much. The enemy is a pro at distorting, distracting, and changing our focus. He hates alignment, especially to the Great Commission.

We have run into opposition and hindrances. We've had misunderstandings about our purpose. Our families have been—and continue to be—challenged when we are on the road. While we haven't faced shipwreck quite yet, we have dealt with illness, confusion, and a lot of outright closed doors.

And you will too as you embark on the journey of aligning with God's mission for your life and church.

Leaders, it's time to take Paul's words in Ephesians 6:13–17 seriously and put on the full armor of God and stand strong. We need to put on the belt of truth, the last 10 percent of truth, to sober us. We need the breastplate of righteousness to guard our hearts and the gospel of peace to center our lives. We need the shield of faith to protect us from spiritual attacks and doubts and the helmet of salvation to guide our thinking. Finally, we need the sword of the Spirit to help us stay on offense.

Paul concludes this instruction by emphasizing the importance of prayer as a vital component in utilizing this spiritual armor effectively.

We must proactively and routinely pray and fast over this work from the start. Let's double down on equipping ourselves and praying for protection and power—and ask others to pray with us!

Reason #2:
Productive collaboration is difficult to foster.

Collaboration is critical to alignment.

One of the great mysteries (and miracles) of God's local church strategy is found in its diversity. In the United States alone, there are hundreds of denominations, countless networks, and endless ways you can segment the church universe.

We know the biblical principles and best practices of alignment work around the US, all over the world, and in other languages. We've seen it. We've led it. And we've learned from it. The church is the church, and the biblical fundamentals apply to it no matter what make or model you lead.

However, the diversity of local church expressions creates both great strength and unique challenges when it comes to developing synergy, fostering collaboration, and linking arms to reach millions of people.

The strength is found in the wide array of perspectives and experiences. Together we are stronger and we look forward to tapping into this vast insight of our growing network more in the coming years.

The challenges are found in a lack of common language and approach to ministry, an unneeded sense of competition, and an identity that is sometimes rooted in one's tribe more than the mission of Christ.

A well-known, successful, young church leader in one of the nation's largest denominations told us that our movement has the potential to transcend denominationalism. He doesn't want to leave his denominational family of origin; rather, he wants to connect and align as many leaders as he can to the great, evangelistic collaboration going on at Intentional Churches.

This is so encouraging! We want to keep it simple so that anyone, from any background, can join and find value in our community.

Reason #3:
Inward focus and Christian consumerism are powerful forces.

We knew inward focus and Christian consumerism would be challenges. We dedicated a whole chapter of *Intentional Churches* to these challenges, but the problem is worse than we thought.

In our experience, the majority of churches prioritize meeting the needs of the Ninety-Nine over reaching the One. Sometimes, this subtle truth goes unnoticed by the leaders in a church. However, it doesn't take a very long look at the budget, calendar, or website to spot the inward focus.

Translation? When we focus on the Ninety-Nine more than the One, we get pulled out of alignment.

Some churches aren't just selfish and consumeristic; they are suffering from spiritual narcissism. And that's an incredibly hard condition to break.

Experts say narcissism is often incurable. To unwind the selfish worldview of a narcissist, you must address a misguided and malformed identity. The narcissist's very purpose and view of self must come under attack in order to be reformed because his or her needs are at the gravitational center of their personal universe.

A narcissist in your life can cause incredible pain. Imagine a dozen, or a hundred, or a thousand narcissists. Sometimes, the healthiest thing you can do is to cut ties altogether or thank the Lord when they choose to do so themselves.

We're not saying to leave your church. Just keep your perspective clear on what's happening and lovingly challenge any spiritual narcissists. It's a spiritual matter, and God will help you. Stay healthy. And stay convicted.

Superman was the strongest man on Earth, but he had one weakness: kryptonite. He became powerless in its presence. The kryptonite to spiritual narcissism is a focus on reaching the One.

It forces you, and your congregation, to assess everything. You must die to yourself, like Jesus instructed, in order to reach the Ones around you. Your calendar, priorities, and budget must change when the mission of Jesus is at the center of your universe.

This assessment may feel uncomfortable at first. We believe you should use this discomfort or tension to your advantage—and a little bit later, we will show you how. Your instinct as a pastor might be to find and alleviate the tension in the system. But that tension is actually going to help you achieve radical alignment. Soon you'll see how.

You need to understand that the possibility of inward focus is real. Count the cost, measure your own heart, and prayerfully prepare. There will be pushback from the consumeristic, and potentially narcissistic, Ninety-Nine. Get ready to use these motivations to get and stay on mission.

Be honest but don't get caught off guard. This is a big issue and our community is here to support you.

> *Search me, O God, and know my heart;*
> *test me and know my anxious thoughts.*
> *Point out anything in me that offends you,*
> *and lead me along the path of everlasting life.*
> —Psalm 139:23–24

CHALLENGING DISCOVERY #2:

Ideas About Church Leadership Are All Over the Map

We have found again and again that members of church leadership teams, including elders and even congregants, have differing definitions for key matters in their church.

Often, the mission, vision, and strategies of the church, along with the roles involved, are individually and uniquely understood. Each leader, team member, and believer creates their own definitions.

If you don't believe us, put a dozen leaders and congregants together and simply ask them to define *discipleship*. Or *evangelism*. Or *the purpose of the church*. You can imagine the array of answers.

- *Discipleship* is defined as strict biblical education according to one leader. To another, it means life-on-life mentoring and shadowing another believer.

- *Evangelism* to one leader is teaching everyone how to draw the "bridge illustration" on a napkin, or share Walter Scott's five-finger sermon. To another, it equates to a strong emphasis on world missions.

- *The purpose of the church*, according to some leaders, is to serve our communities and help the oppressed. To others, it is to proclaim the Gospel, take a stand on social matters, or offer hope and healing to those in need.

While all of these partial definitions can be true, they can also be in conflict with one another. This can create tremendous inefficiency and sideways energy. You'll never be an Intentional Church if you don't unify, clarify, and declare definitions.

In technical terms, we have found that embracing what it means to be an Intentional Church—a One-aware, activated, and radically aligned church—means pushing hard to align theology, ecclesiology, and missiology.

Theology is . . .
your understanding of God.

Ecclesiology is . . .
your understanding of the church.

Missiology is . . .
your understanding of the role of the church in the world.

In simpler terms, it will be hard to make more and better disciples and double your kingdom impact if this thing called the "church" doesn't make sense to everyone in the same way!

We have coined this as a "leadership worldview." A leadership worldview is the framework you use for making decisions. It includes the guiding beliefs and underlying assumptions you lean on as you lead your church.

We all have a leadership worldview, whether we've thought about it or not. It's always there, running in the background. We want to show you how to bring it into the open, define it clearly, and use it to create radical alignment.

It's not easy to shape a worldview. It takes patience as a leader. Sometimes, you are unwinding an old worldview and replacing it with a new one. Other times, you are teaching a new worldview where little was established before. There's always someone new to onboard and teach—and sometimes, it involves fending off someone fighting for their former understanding.

Regardless, it takes time and perseverance.

There's no replacement for the reps it will take and no way to overestimate the value in aligning your church's leadership worldview. It will create tremendous synergy and pave the road for you to become an Intentional Church.

CHALLENGING DISCOVERY #3:
Impulsive Leadership Tendencies Are Worse Than We Thought

Most of the churches we've worked with have advanced the Great Commission using the Intentional Churches Toolbox. However, not all of them have chosen to install it fully as their organizational operating system.

There are many reasons, but perhaps the most common is the fact that church leaders can be impatient, and sometimes impulsive, in their commitments. If you are going to unify your church's worldview of leadership and life and install the Intentional Churches Toolbox, it's going to take some time.

In *Intentional Churches*, we attributed this impulsiveness to a few factors—a deep conviction, a strong sense of urgency, and a glut of information and quality options.

Many church leaders think: *Why not read as many books, try as many things, and go to as many conferences as possible until I find something that works?*

This is simply not a great strategy, if one at all. We can confirm it is leading to the unintended consequences of diminishing confidence, discouragement, and outright fear in some leaders.

At the same time, the irony is not lost on us that we have written a book, created the Intentional Churches Toolbox, and started a conference! We have been seen as the silver bullet solution, and we have also been rebuffed because we aren't.

Our aim is to free you from the maddening or unproductive cycle of silver-bullet solutions and impulsive approaches to church leadership. We want to help you think clearly through every option and guide you in making leadership decisions that create and maintain alignment to the mission.

Here's the logic (it's scriptural):

- all things are possible, but not everything is expedient
- become what you need to become in order to reach some
- at the same time, be ready to test and approve what is right

We are building a community of like-minded leaders who, together, will be able to test and approve what is right—what helps one another build a One-aware, activated, and radically aligned church.

Leadership shouldn't be a randomized series of decisions for an Intentional Church. It should be a series of Holy Spirit–driven commitments that are taken seriously and held loosely, because He can and will do immeasurably more than you hope or think when you align to His mission.

CHALLENGING DISCOVERY #4:
Evangelism Has Been Unlinked From Discipleship

> Unlink = *Break the connection between something and something else.*

We're not sure how it happened, and it's kind of hard to believe. In many circles, evangelism and discipleship are completely unlinked. Evangelism is a distant second to the increasingly popular topic of discipleship.

Even worse, a false dichotomy has been created. Some believe you have to choose whether you are going to be a church focused on discipleship or evangelism. We even had one church pray for thirty days about this decision!

What?

Evangelism and discipleship have been separated when they are inextricably linked. Can you see how this contributes to misalignment?

How can you be a disciple without evangelizing? How can you evangelize without being a disciple? How can you make a disciple without them first being reached? How can you claim you're a disciple without reaching someone?

Pause. Deep breath. Maybe read those questions again.

This is a weird one, but it's so true. Aren't both things key elements of the Great Commission—the mission of every believer and church?

> *Therefore, go and make disciples of all the nations, baptizing them in the name of the Father and the Son and the Holy Spirit. Teach these new disciples to obey all the commands I have given you. And be sure of this: I am with you always, even to the end of the age.*
>
> —Matthew 28:19–20

So, how did this happen? We have developed some theories from our work about how these two very important topics have become unlinked.

Theory #1:
Overreaction

There is an epidemic of undeveloped, or poorly developed, Christians, especially in the United States. The reasons can be argued, but the stats are clear.

According to the Barna Group:

- Only 45 percent of Christians say their relationship with Jesus brings them deep joy.

- Only 41 percent of Christians say faith impacts the way they live their daily life.

- Only 33 percent of Christians say they are willing to pass along to others what they have learned in life.

Our friends at the Renew.org Network, a discipleship ministry, estimate that 80 percent of Christians are infants in their faith, or possibly not even saved! Wow.

You can google your own stats although you probably don't need to. This reality has created a couple of potential overreactions.

First, some leaders are swinging the conversation so far toward the development of the believers that they've left the evangelism conversation behind. The irony is that this could cause the very problem they are attempting to correct—the forgetting of the lost and the creation of an inward focus. We've seen it.

Another reason some churches overreact is poor vision casting and change management.

The church we mentioned earlier that needed to pray for thirty days about whether to focus on evangelism *or* discipleship had been through a terrible time of turmoil. A lot had changed overnight in the name of reaching the One. Church members weren't given a chance to ask questions and work through the reasons for the changes. The idea of reaching the One had been weaponized. If you weren't on board, you were kicked off board!

That's not cool. You can understand the overreaction.

We believe the answer is in a loving but healthy imbalance toward the One in planning and decision-making. Our Great Commission Engine tool has a recommended 70/30 imbalance toward the One as you use it for evaluation. We'll tell you more about tools later.

The reason it works is because the Ninety-Nine naturally add a good dose of self-focus to the equation. By unbalancing your focus, you can, ironically, balance the outcomes of both evangelism and discipleship. It might be counterintuitive but it's true.

Theory #2:
Misdiagnosis

Many leaders have sensed a problem. Their churches aren't growing and reaching people. The voices of the selfish Ninety-Nine are growing louder. Something must be done!

Your natural inclination may be to think the solution is a matter of deeper teaching and discipleship. Similar to the last theory, this response is understandable.

Sometimes, the one missing ingredient is a focus on the lost.

We worked with one church that was convinced they were going to disciple their Ninety-Nine back to caring about the lost and reaching people again. Instead, the church turned more and more inward and stayed in decline. They were literally discipling their way toward closing.

Again, the remedy is as simple as becoming more One-aware and activated in everything you do. It's a powerful solution.

Theory #3:
Lack of Faith

This shows up all over the place.

Lack of faith was particularly evident during the COVID-19 pandemic. Many churches turned grossly inward at the fear of losing the Ninety-Nine and completely left the idea of evangelism behind. The One was temporarily or, in some cases, completely forgotten.

As church leaders, we have a sincere desire to see people follow Jesus and increasingly surrender to His lordship. We know the transformative difference that following him can make in someone's life and how it can impact a family for generations. But it's easy to think it's our responsibility, not God's, to bring about lasting transformation.

In one of our recent workshops, a leader mentioned that you shouldn't think about replication until the original is in good shape. You don't want to replicate something that isn't ready yet. Put in spiritual terms, an immature believer doesn't make a good disciple-maker.

This caused a decent amount of thought initially. The admonition came from a good place.

However, it didn't take long to realize this could also be used as an excuse. God is in the business of using the imperfect to propagate His cause. Think about the original versions of David, Peter, and Paul. Or all the disciples, for that matter. What a mess they were!

It was Paul who wrote these words in First and Second Corinthians:

> *I didn't use lofty words and impressive wisdom to tell you God's secret plan. For I decided that while I was with you I would forget everything except Jesus Christ, the one who was crucified.... It is not that we think we are qualified to do anything on our own. Our qualification comes from God. He has enabled us to be ministers of his new covenant.*
>
> —1 Corinthians 2:1-2, 2 Corinthians 5-6

Wow! Even the apostle Paul knew he was inadequate to share the gospel. We must rely on God's help.

You shouldn't wait until you have perfect disciples, or a perfect discipleship plan, to teach your church about the primacy of reaching the lost sheep. In fact, it should be the first order of business in disciple-making.

Teaching people to reach people is risky. It's messy.

In another case, in a church learning to be One-aware and activated, a very well-meaning deacon raised the caution that by inviting the lost to participate in the kids' ministry, it would become filled with the children of unsaved folks. "They would be rubbing shoulders with our kids," he said. After a minute of reflection, he concluded, "Well, I suppose that's the way it should be."

It took that deacon a special kind of courage to get to that realization.

God is in the business of using the imperfect to accomplish His will. He is in charge, going before and after us. He's got this. Embracing that mindset will take courage for some.

In the end, the great irony is that by unlinking evangelism from discipleship, no matter the reason, you are likely contributing to the inward focus of your church.

We still believe it. One of God's greatest tools to grow the Ninety-Nine is a focus on the Ones yet to be reached—even during a global pandemic, when our church's doors are closed, when change is hard, or when we risk a mess.

A focus on the One challenges all of the right assumptions and helps us build incredibly healthy churches.

CHALLENGING DISCOVERY #5:
We Have Institutionalized the Great Commission

For some reason, we have convinced ourselves that buildings, church services, and programs advance the gospel.

The reality? They can't and don't accomplish the Great Commission.

People do.

We call this *institutional thinking,* and it is a tremendous headwind to advancing the One-aware and activated church. With this mindset, you value . . .

Transactions Over Transformation. It feels like . . . hitting the goal is the win. Speed is of the essence and sometimes the addiction. Inputs matter more than outcomes.

Programs Over Process. It looks like . . . ministries, events, and programs are the reason we have a church calendar and a budget—and staff! Having the event *is* the win.

Responsibilities Over Relationships. It sounds like . . . "do your job" or "that's not my job!" Staffing ratios drive decisions. You aren't asking one another, "How's it going with your One?"

Here's some further evidence we've encountered that institutional thinking has taken over.

The view of what it means to serve in the church is skewed. We see our (and others') contribution as filling a requirement or checking a box of obligation. No thought is given to the personal fulfillment of the Great Commission.

It may be worse for the professional pastorate.

Often, pastors and staff are seen as doers, not developers. You can name the various functions in the church—administering the sacraments, teaching, running the soundboard, leading kids' ministry, on and on it goes. These leaders are expected to accomplish the Great Commission on behalf of the Ninety-Nine instead of first living it out personally and then equipping the Ninety-Nine to do the same.

The Bible is very clear about this matter. The church is an equipping organization. This is how He has blessed, gifted, and organized His Church.

> Now these are the gifts Christ gave to the church: the apostles, the prophets, the evangelists, and the pastors and teachers. Their responsibility is to equip God's people to do his work and build up the church, the body of Christ.
>
> —Ephesians 4:11–12

So, what do we do? How do we break the institutionalization of the Great Commission?

Test and approve. Test and approve.

This is important to the process of radical alignment.

We should audit every event, ministry, program, role, and job description against its Great Commission purpose. What does this look like in practice?

Ask questions and seek the truth.

- How does this (event, ministry, program, or role) help us make more and better disciples?

- How does this (event, ministry, program, or role) inspire, equip, and activate the Ninety-Nine to reach the One?

- How are those involved in this (event, ministry, program, or role) becoming more like Jesus?

These are some tough realities to process and you probably saw yourself in there somewhere.

We also have some very encouraging news.

For Individual Reflection and Application:

1. Which of the five challenging discoveries resonates most strongly with your personal experience in ministry? Why?

2. Do you struggle more with impulsiveness, looking for "silver bullet" solutions, or with being distracted from the mission? How can you address this?

3. Consider the concept of "spiritual narcissism" in churches. How can you guard against making your own needs or your church's comfort the center of your ministry universe?

For Team Discussion and Interaction:

1. Which of the challenges have you experienced in ministry? Which challenge has hit you the hardest in leadership? Discuss as a team.

2. Examine the theories about why evangelism and discipleship have become unlinked. Which theory best explains what you've observed in your church or community?

AN INTENTIONAL CHURCH STORY

From Consumer Mentality to Kingdom Builders: How Beulahland Bible Church Discovered Radical Alignment

When Jessica Sayles lost her mother and brother within ten months, she watched her father drift away from church despite never losing his love for Jesus. What she didn't know was that a woman in her congregation had chosen her father as her "One"—praying intentionally for his return. Today, because of that woman's commitment to radical alignment with the Great Commission, Jessica's dad has found his church home again.

This transformation didn't happen by accident. It began when Senior Pastor Dr. Carlos Kelly read *Intentional Churches* during his annual vision retreat. "I literally read it in one day," he recalls. "It was like one of those aha moments. This was exactly what we had been praying for."

For twenty-six years, Beulahland Bible Church had preached the Great Commission annually, but Pastor Kelly discovered a sobering truth: "I didn't realize how many of our church members had a consumer mentality. When they came to church, it was 'What's in it for me?' as opposed to 'What can I do?'"

The solution required brutal honesty. A fourteen-person team from across two campuses spent months deconstructing everything they thought was wonderful about their church. "We've had some knock-down, drag-out meetings where we went under the hood, seeing how we *really* were as a church," said Director of Assimilation Sam Reid.

The process revealed sacred cows that weren't leading them to reach the One. They revamped their website, which had been designed for insiders rather than the lost. They developed a crystal-clear mission: "We make disciples."

But the real transformation came through personal conviction. Executive Pastor Greg Holt realized he had "unlinked evangelism and discipleship," treating altar calls as endpoints rather than starting points. Reid discovered they were trying to create "Christian experts within a ten-to-fifteen-minute time frame" instead of walking alongside new believers.

Now, eighteen months into their journey, Beulahland is witnessing the multiplication effect. Pastor Holt's vision is simple but revolutionary: "If one person took one disciple per year and taught that disciple how to make a disciple, over five years that's thirty-one new disciples. That's the multiplier that creates exponential growth."

The church is still becoming radically aligned, but the evidence is clear. As Sam Reid puts it: "When you share the Gospel and make disciples, not only are you pouring out, but you're getting back tenfold. Your church is going to grow—not just in numbers, but spiritually and healthy."

The question for every pastor remains: Are you ready to move your congregation from consumers to kingdom builders?

Read Beulahland's
Full Story Here

CHAPTER 3

5 Encouraging Discoveries

In the last chapter, we looked at some challenges we *all* face and how we are learning together to overcome them. It's important to learn from both the challenges and the victories when you reflect.

In the victories, there's additional learning to be had and an opportunity for celebration. There's also a chance to reinforce and expand on what you know is working.

ENCOURAGING DISCOVERY #1:

Our Unifying Theory of Church Growth Is Real

Let's begin with a couple of references from our first book, *Intentional Churches*.

> *In the early 1900s, Albert Einstein developed the theory of relativity. For now, it remains the best explanation of how the universe works when it comes to energy, expansion, and masses. . . . You don't have to create something new to have lasting impact. You only need to interpret the dynamics and learn how they fundamentally apply to life.*
>
> *So how did God design the church? Could there be a unified theory that would help us all understand how to lead our churches? How to be more intentional? If so, we could all get back to basics and understand God's intent for the local church. . . . We submit there are scriptural foundations that point us to a unifying theory for church leadership and growth.*[1]

---

[1] Bart Rendel and Doug Parks, *Intentional Churches: How Implementing an Operating System Clarifies Vision, Improves Decision Making, and Stimulates Growth* (Thomas Nelson, 2020), xxviii.

Our foundational Scriptures for this unifying theory are found in Matthew 28:19–20, Acts 1:8, Acts 2:42–47, Luke 15, and Ephesians 4.

If these foundations are universally true and applicable to every church, we can build an operating system that would create incredible outcomes for the accomplishment of the Great Commission.

So, what is an organizational operating system?

> *An operating system is the filter through which inputs and outputs are processed. . . . It's a comprehensive set of leadership tools that have broad applications built on unifying biblical foundations. It's a system that makes the hardware (the gospel, people, buildings, and finances) and the software (today's and tomorrow's ministry strategies and solutions) work together incredibly well today and tomorrow. It's a system that eliminates the search for the next silver-bullet strategy.*[2]

Our operating system is working around the United States and even the world. The model, tools, and processes need translation, but they work. With the help of our community, we have created a customizable template based on biblical fundamentals. It's adaptable to any church, as evidenced by the proliferation of its use in such a variety of contexts.

In Vietnam, there is a flourishing church reaching the One in record numbers. It's one of the largest churches now in Hanoi. In New Brunswick, Canada, there is a church that baptized the same number of people in one year as its average attendance from the previous year.

---

[2] Rendel and Parks, xxx.

In Florida, there is a megachurch completely overhauling its newly renovated campus to become more One-aware and activated. In Wichita, Kansas, and Newburgh, Indiana, there are churches radically aligning their boards, leadership, and congregations by training every believer how to pray for and reach their personal One.

When you focus on biblical authority, unity, and the Great Commission by putting the Ones to be reached first, incredible things can happen—in you, your church, and your community.

It's working all over, and the outcomes are palpable. They align with our original dreams of the Intentional Churches community collaborating to reach more people for Christ because they are using the same leadership toolbox.

Synergy. Churches are using the same underlying processes and language. This generates the ability to collaborate and discover new and improved solutions at a faster rate than ever before.

Timeliness. Solutions are being created based on an understanding of how the church was meant to work. These solutions are not silver bullets but rather smart bullets designed to accomplish the church's mission in today's context.

Repeatability. The rhythms and routines involved in an operating system are creating unparalleled gains in effort and efficiency. The Great Commission impact is greater than ever before.

Adaptability. Times are changing rapidly. With the Intentional Churches Toolbox as a foundation, the church is applying solutions at the right time in the most effective way. Our dream is that churches in our movement will become some of the most adaptable organizations on the planet.

Predictability. With the growing development of our learning community, churches no longer have to wonder if solutions are going to work or not. Crowdsourcing the right solutions and smart development is greatly reducing the guesswork in church leadership.

Alignment. The unifying model allows teams and departments to operate in a similar way. Common understanding, shared language, and a conviction to reach the One are being created. Ministry leaders are on the same page, helping one another be more effective regardless of their roles.

Confidence. Great operating systems just work. You turn on the power, boot up the software, and are ready to go. You don't question the mechanics. You just create the right inputs, and the results flow. This is happening when it comes to the Great Commission.

Connection. Churches from all backgrounds are finding a home—a place of common understanding, encouragement, and inspiration. The common language and approach to ministry is creating unity.

So, what do these churches have in common?

Patrick Lencioni's framework in *The Ideal Team Player* aligns well. We've found these churches are:

Humble. They realize they are just one church among many in God's redemptive, miraculous plan. No one church can do it all. They know we are better together, and they don't have a prideful, must-be-invented-here mentality. They are willing to learn from others and help by sharing their best ideas.

Hungry. They want more—not for their own glory, but for God's. They fully believe in the incredible potential of the church (because of the power of the gospel and the Holy Spirit) and want to see it released. They yearn for God's guidance and presence and want to follow Him each and every day.

Smart. They major on the biblical fundamentals of church leadership and continue to get reps in them. They use team-based tools to mine out the wisdom of the group with the Spirit's power. They are always learning and improving. Their EQ, or emotional intelligence, matches their IQ as they create a healthy church by simply focusing on reaching the One.

We want and need you in this community!

ENCOURAGING DISCOVERY #2:

The Future Is Bright in the Hands of Young and Old Leaders

Thanks to David and Kristin Miller, founders of Leadership Pathway, for helping us put words to what we are sensing and seeing. And more importantly, what to do about it.

The future of the Intentional Churches movement shines bright in the hands of young leaders, but older leaders play a critical role. As you'll see, radical alignment requires an agility and willingness to adapt in a way that comes naturally to young leaders. You must commit yourself to understanding them and building a multigenerational leadership team.

We've seen younger leaders go further, move faster, and do more with the Intentional Churches Toolbox. You need them in your mix! Here's some help in understanding this current crop of new stewards we must raise up.

Dr. Tim Elmore's work on the next generation of leaders is insightful. He says they are fundamentally different from their predecessors. Unlike earlier generations who waited their turn, today's young leaders are digital natives who won't wait to be given permission—they create their own opportunities.

They are also ready to bring a transformative approach to ministry and organizational leadership. They aren't interested in perpetuating outdated systems or tolerating unhealthy workplace environments. They prioritize healthy boundaries and reject the burnout culture of previous generations.

Where older leaders have normalized overwork and constant availability, young leaders demand balance and meaningful engagement. This isn't a weakness but a strength that could fundamentally transform your team's culture.

Healthy, older leaders have a crucial role to play in the future. The true potential of these young leaders will only be realized through intentional mentorship. Older leaders must approach this generation with cultural humility, much like a missiologist engaging an unfamiliar culture. This means sitting with young leaders and understanding their customs and language. It's about listening, learning together, and mutually growing.

We need the radical alignment of young and old!

As Kristin emphasizes, leadership development is not about training but about coaching. This means creating environments where young leaders are:

- Spiritually formed
- Equipped with critical soft skills
- Given genuine ownership and opportunities to lead
- Supported with mental wellness strategies
- Engaged in meaningful developmental conversations

We need every Intentional Church to embrace this approach of intentional, compassionate leadership development. You must invest consistently—not just once or twice, but persistently over the years.

Imagine the power of aligning young and old leaders to the Great Commission. Imagine a multi-generational team leading a One-aware and activated church. They will have a shared purpose and use their differences in leadership as a strength. Radically aligning young and old leaders is imperative for your church.

ENCOURAGING DISCOVERY #3:

It Starts With You

We weren't at this for very long before we realized there is an incredibly personal side to everything we teach and equip. In fact, if it doesn't become personally impactful to you as a disciple, it will be an empty, powerless leadership exercise with limited and short-lived kingdom gains.

You'll soon see the full role *you* play in radical alignment.

Here's what we mean.

One of our primary tools is the Great Commission Engine. It takes the foundational Scriptures from Matthew 28:19–12, Acts 2:42–47, Luke 15, and Ephesians 4 and combines them into a simple, useful model for planning and evaluation.

> **And they devoted themselves to the apostles' teaching and the fellowship, to the breaking of bread and the prayers.**
>
> Acts 2:42

There are six parts to the model. These components power the Gospel impact of every church. Each component has a meaningful organizational application that begins with a powerful personal application.

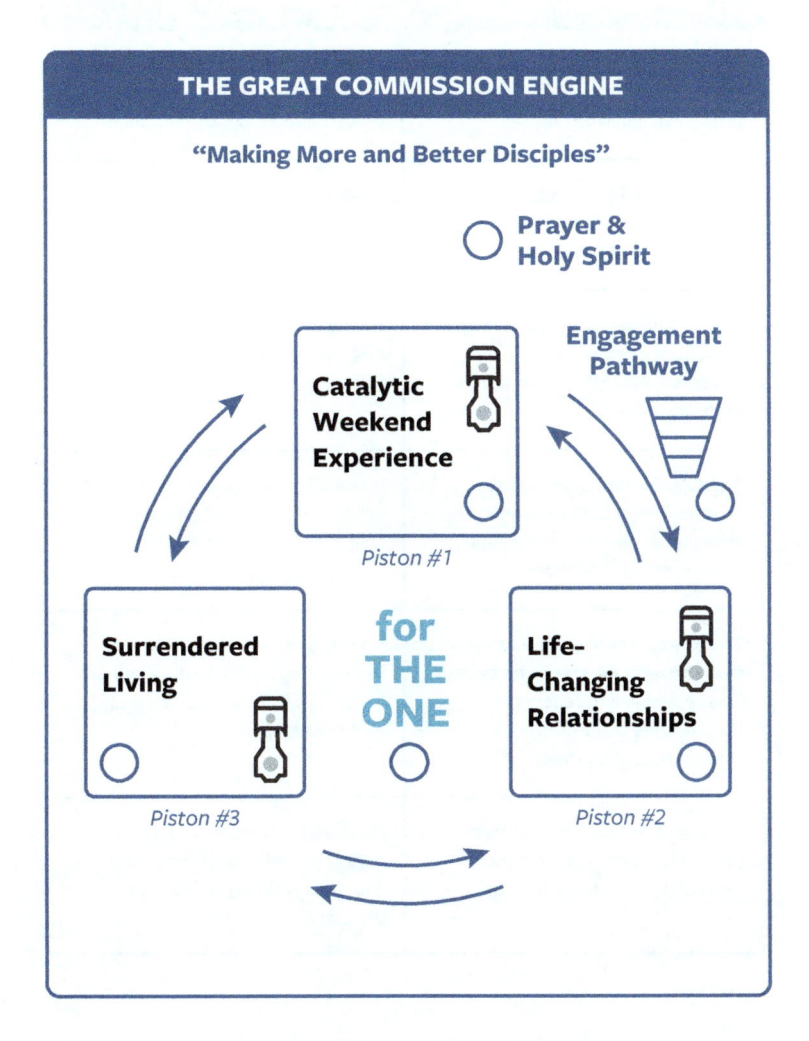

THE GREAT COMMISSION ENGINE

"Making More and Better Disciples"

Prayer & Holy Spirit

Catalytic Weekend Experience
Piston #1

Engagement Pathway

Life-Changing Relationships
Piston #2

Surrendered Living
Piston #3

for THE ONE

ORGANIZATIONAL APPLICATION	PERSONAL ASSESSMENT
Piston 1 is The Gathering. The power comes from being together, preaching, and worship.	What's your engagement look like in committing to The Gathering, powerful teaching, and worship?
Piston 2 is Life-Changing Relationships. The power comes from community.	What's your engagement look like when it comes to living in rich community?
Piston 3 is Surrendered Living. The power comes from an increasing commitment to the lordship of Christ.	How are you challenging yourself to grow in your surrender and commitment to the Lord?
The Crankshaft is the center around which it all revolves. The primacy of reaching the One must be considered in all things.	Is reaching your One at the center of your life and involvement in your church?
The Engagement Pathway is an ever-present connections system. It's the simple and sequential way the One gets connected to Jesus, your church, and others.	Do you have an Engagement Pathway in your life that helps you build a relationship and connect with the One?
Proactive Prayer has a stated plan. It is there to protect your plans and power them forward.	Do you have a proactive plan to regularly pray, especially when it comes to your engagement of the One?

You get the picture, right? Leaders go first when it comes to making commitments.

In Philippians 3:17, Paul emphasizes this point when he says, *"Dear brothers and sisters, pattern your lives after mine, and learn from those who follow our example."*

Have you gone first? How does your personal engagement in the Great Commission Engine look?

Shelter Cove Church in Modesto, California, uses the Great Commission Engine as a tool to measure the personal radical alignment of each leadership team member. What would happen if your staff meetings started with a simple question: "How's it going with your One?"

The same principle of personal alignment is also true for our Acts 1:8 tool.

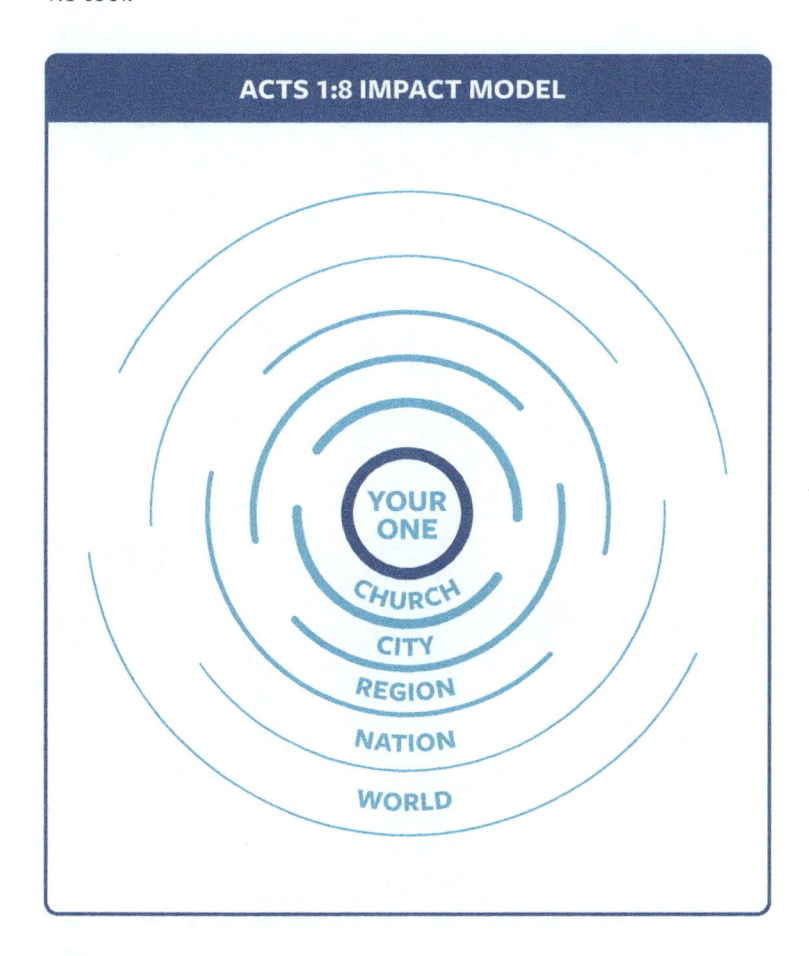

ACTS 1:8 IMPACT MODEL

- YOUR ONE
- CHURCH
- CITY
- REGION
- NATION
- WORLD

Organizational. This tool teaches that the first focus of your ministry should be on your home base—your Jerusalem or Antioch. Too many churches have lost sight of focusing on reaching the One in their home base. This results in lost impact that sometimes goes away forever.

Personal. It also teaches that each of us has a "personal Jerusalem or Antioch" of impact. Our impact centers on the lives of our personal Ones, and even the lives of the Ones connected to our Ones!

Another tool we use is the Relational Reach Zone.

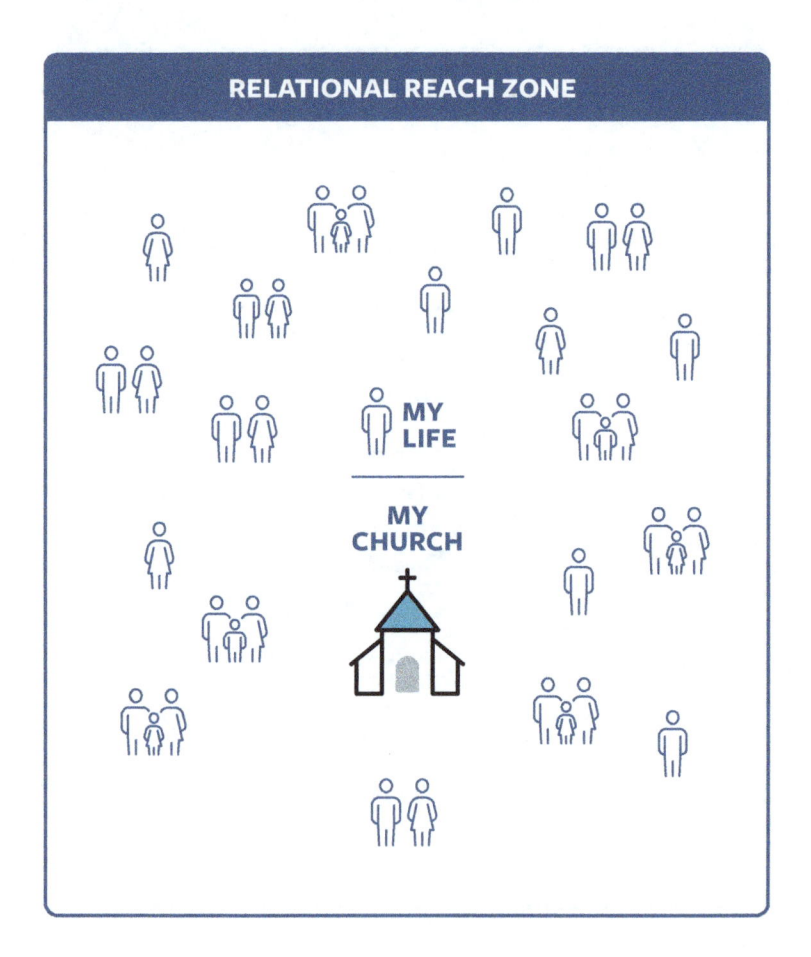

RELATIONAL REACH ZONE

MY LIFE

MY CHURCH

Organizational. This tool teaches that each and every church has unique potential for spiritual impact. The potential sits in the relational networks connected to your church. These networks are unique to your church, eliminating the need to compete for the involvement of another church's Ninety-Nine.

Personal. The same can be said of you and your personal relational networks. You have a one-of-a-kind relational reach zone. It's geographical, spiritual, and relational. Your reach zone is where you live, work, and play. Ones are all around you! Who is your One?

If you want a practical exercise in alignment, pull out a sheet of paper and draw stick figures like we have represented. Label the boundaries *north, south, east,* and *west* of where you live, work, and regularly play. Now write the names of Ones who are in geographical, spiritual, or relational proximity to you next to the stick figures. With a little thought and prayer, you'll be amazed at the opportunities for gospel impact right around you.

What next?

Pray for at least one genuine relationship to emerge from that list if it hasn't already. God will lead you to your One(s) and them to you.

Radically aligned leaders know and understand their personal relational reach zone. They review it regularly and pray for God-borne intersections daily.

A Simple Prayer. Personal radical alignment can begin with a simple prayer of availability. "God, I'm available. What would you have me do today to align myself and my church to your mission?" He will never let that request go unanswered—He will answer in big and small ways.

We started Intentional Churches with a similar prayer. Similar to Isaiah's request, we said, "Here we are, send us." That's another simple prayer that will spin your life and ministry around.

God put in both of us a deep desire to serve in the local church—we will always be in it, with it, around it, and loving on it. It is our holy affliction. We are constrained in a good way to see this mission of alignment through.

As we left our jobs at our beloved churches to do this work on a full-time basis, He provided again and again in ways we couldn't expect. He opened doors and offered encouragement on a just-in-time basis. But most importantly, He convicted us deeply about living out the very ideals we teach others.

It's difficult to teach a team about the importance of leading a One-aware and activated church if you aren't living a One-aware and activated life yourself. If we really believe in this radical alignment thing, and that it begins with the leader, then it has to also begin with us!

Ask us about our Ones if you get the chance.

Sometimes, maybe right now, the most powerful thing you can do is stop and pray a simple prayer of Great Commission availability. Get ready for Him to move in your life and church.

Yes, this discovery is about how an organizational toolbox must become a personal toolbox as well. Otherwise, it will likely be just another random attempt to grow your church, but it's so much more than that.

ENCOURAGING DISCOVERY #4:

(Yes, It Starts With You, but . . .) You Can't Do It Alone

A friend of ours says, "Church leadership is a team sport." And he is so right. Too often, leaders try to go it alone and end up isolated, doubt-filled, and fearful.

It wasn't meant to be that way.

Over the past dozen years, we've discovered the power of collaboration. We've established a common framework for use in church leadership that includes the common language and approaches we've been sharing in this book.

Today, we are seeing the benefits of coming together to advance the Great Commission. We are on the cusp of realizing the vision of "thousands of churches collaborating to reach millions."

One hurdle we've encountered is not having the ability to be together very often. We've seen synergy come from our Facebook communities, training events, and conference, but it's time to take our collaboration to the next level.

The collaboration needs to be 24/7, on-demand, and virtual. The movement must go digital if it's going to be owned by its participants.

This is why we are launching the Intentional Churches community called One Community.

One Community will first and foremost be a space for the movement's leadership and participants to collaborate and learn from one another. For the vision to be accomplished, it requires a home base for advancement.

A learning community is a group of people who actively engage in collaborative learning with shared goals and interests. It's a place where participants learn from each other's experiences, share resources, and work together to enhance their knowledge and skills in specific areas.

It's characterized by:

- A culture of continuous learning and knowledge sharing
- Regular interaction and dialogue between members
- A collective focus on building understanding and expertise
- A safe environment for questions, discussion, and exploration
- Support for both individual and team development

It does all of this through social interaction, shared discovery, and mutual support rather than a one-way knowledge transfer. It's owned by those involved!

Our community will be a place where you can find your people, collaborate, and gather insights. There will be a lot of stories and encouragement. And ultimately, we will help one another lead One-aware, activated, and radically aligned lives and churches.

Do you have a community? If not, you need one. It's so important.

ENCOURAGING DISCOVERY #5:

Radical Alignment Is the Answer

Over the years, we've come to realize leadership teams can't and don't create lasting evangelistic alignment in a church alone. It's going to take something called *radical alignment*.

There is a way to create a One-aware and activated church that stands the test of time. It's biblical and powerful. It's going to take the transformation of every believer, including you and your team, and ultimately involve all of your church.

Let's get into *Radical Alignment* . . .

What is it?
Why is it radical?
How does it work?
How do you make it happen?
How do you make it stick?

For Individual Reflection and Application:

1. If the people who know you were honest, would they say you need to grow the most in being humble, hungry, or smart? What is one step you could take to grow in that characteristic?

2. Consider the personal applications of the Great Commission Engine components. Where are you strongest and weakest in your personal engagement?

3. Reflect on your personal "relational reach zone." Who are the specific Ones in your geographical, spiritual, and relational proximity? Commit to begin praying for them daily.

For Team Discussion and Interaction:

1. Discuss the importance of multigenerational leadership teams. How can your team better understand and integrate both young and older leaders?

2. Share with each other: "How's it going with your One?" How might it help if you made this question a regular part of your team meetings?

AN INTENTIONAL CHURCH STORY

From Survival Mode to Strategic Growth:
How Radical Alignment Transformed a Missouri Church

Connection Point Church in Jackson, Missouri, proves that when churches radically align with the Great Commission, God moves in extraordinary ways. What started as a church in "survival mode" has become the largest congregation between St. Louis and Memphis, all while maintaining their core mission: "We want to see God do a work that only Jesus can get credit for."

The Power of One-Awareness
Pastor Chris Vaught's team discovered the transformative impact of identifying their "One" persona—a 28-year-old male and a hurting 27-year-old female struggling to find purpose. This laser focus revolutionized every ministry area, from marriage programs to discipleship groups. The results? Dramatic growth among the unchurched, with prayer team members regularly fielding questions like, "He mentioned John 3:16. What is that?" The church has baptized approximately 250 people annually for several consecutive years.

Strategic Alignment Through Intentional Church Model
Using the Intentional Church Toolbox, CPC achieved what Ministry Strategist Lisa Vaught calls "radical alignment." The Great Commission Engine became their north star, with staff members teaching it monthly because "if you can teach it, you remember it." This approach broke down ministry silos and maintained their 70 percent lean toward reaching the One, even as they experienced explosive growth.

The Ripple Effect
Initially, some worried that targeting younger demographics would alienate older members. Instead, CPC discovered the "ripple effect"—as young adults found Christ, their parents and

grandparents followed. While their target demographic dropped by ten years, the church now hosts more 50-, 60-, and 70-year-olds than ever before.

The Leadership Lesson
Pastor Chris emphasizes the choice every church faces: "You can either be afraid of the mission, building your strategy around personal preferences and comfort, or you can build a strategy around the Great Commission." CPC chose the latter, resulting in confidence-driven ministry that expects God's blessing.

For pastors seeking sustainable growth without compromising mission, CPC demonstrates that radical alignment isn't about changing the message—it's about strategically contextualizing the Great Commission for your community while maintaining unwavering focus on reaching the lost.

Read Connection Point's Full Story Here

CHAPTER 4

One Solution

There is one theme running through all of our discoveries. We need a new (or old) kind of alignment to the mission.

ALIGNMENT

Think about the important benefits of alignment and the dangers of misalignment.

Train Tracks

Two simple, aligned metal rails allow a powerful locomotive to move with speed and efficiency. It takes a while to build the track, but the benefit is worth the effort.

There is no doubt that misalignment of the tracks will lead to derailment and tragedy.

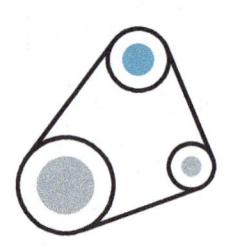

An Engine

The mechanics of an engine are impressive. There are thousands of moving parts that must be perfectly aligned and timed. They are aligned by a simple device called a timing belt or chain. It ensures that all the parts work in harmony and coordination to deliver power to the wheels.

Misalignment will lead to misfiring and, in the worst case, complete engine failure and loss of power.

Wheels

The wheels on a car must periodically be aligned to prevent drift and vibrations. If the wheels are aligned, you can limit distractions and focus your energy on reaching your destination.

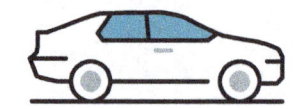

Misalignment will lead to a constant fight to stay on course, and vibrations will eventually tear things apart. Alignment is incredibly important, and the consequences of misalignment can be tragic.

In the church, it seems like alignment should come easily. We have the same mission. We share a vision of heaven and a picture of what it means to follow Jesus. And our values are very similar because they generally come from the Bible and our Christian faith.

We should naturally be on the same page. Right? Not really. In fact, you've probably experienced the opposite.

Here are a few of the symptoms of misalignment:

- Long Meetings
- Lack of Accountability
- Ministry Silos and Isolationism
- Fear and Worry
- Lack of Conversions
- Subjective Evaluation Standards
- Unprioritized Scheduling and Budgeting
- Overcontrol and Micromanagement
- Constant Debate
- Fuzzy Decision-Making
- Purposeless Events and Programs
- Thoughts like "My Ministry, My Budget, My Volunteers"
- Christian Consumerism
- Declining Impact
- Insider or Confusing Language and Definitions
- Disagreement on Priorities
- High Staff-to-Congregant Ratios
- Confusion Over Unity vs. Consensus

Here is what misalignment feels like.

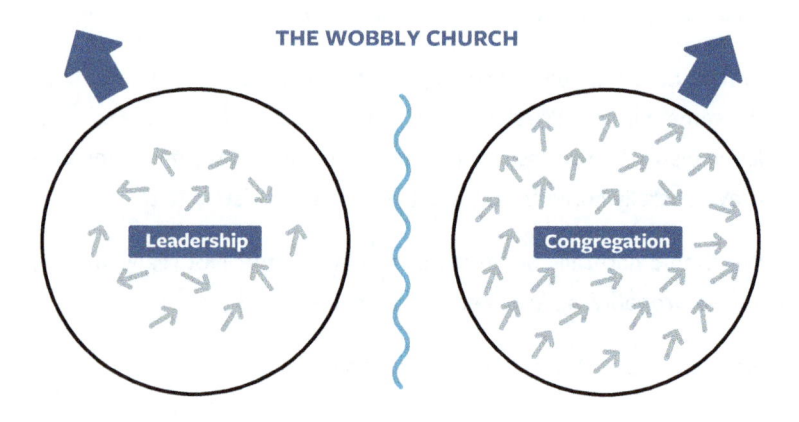

THE WOBBLY CHURCH

The Wobbly Church is unsure of its direction. It wanders to and fro, hunting for direction from the latest fads and programs. The loudest voices or strongest leaders win, but only for a season.

THE STALEMATE CHURCH

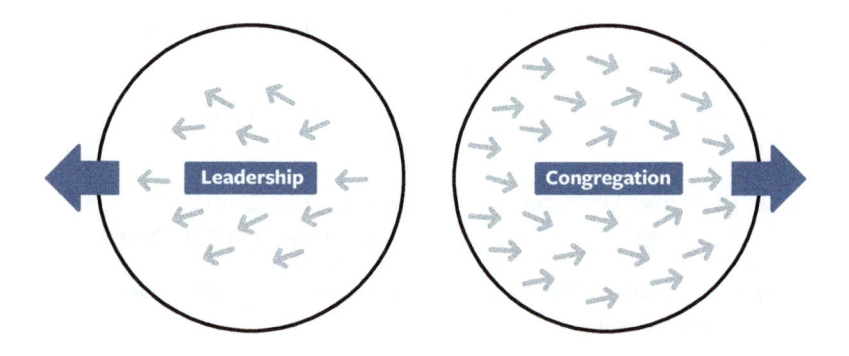

The Stalemate Church is embroiled in senseless battles. Meetings descend into matters of opinion with no definitive conclusions. Often, Christians behave like consumers, pulling the church toward their selfish needs. The status quo is really hard to break.

THE RETREATING CHURCH

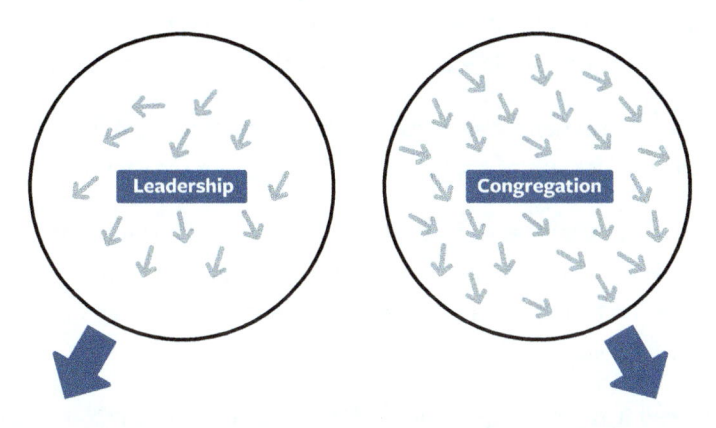

In the Retreating Church, motivations are waning and good intentions are drying up. The leaders and congregation have decided the best days are behind them and the future isn't worth the fight.

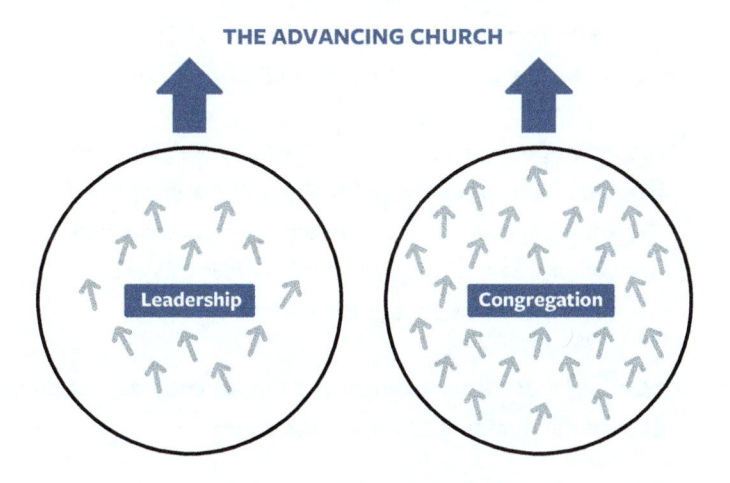

THE ADVANCING CHURCH

Even the Advancing Church needs alignment.

In the Advancing Church, things feel like they are moving in the right direction. Progress is being made, but there may not be real alignment. What feels like alignment is really just the celebration of temporary wins. As intentions change and challenges come, the alignment will wane if the leadership and congregation don't fundamentally, deeply, and personally align with the Great Commission.

Have you experienced any of the effects or characteristics of misalignment in your church? Are you advancing and want the wins to last?

There is an alignment of a different kind—one that is foundational, complete, and permanent. It spreads deeply to the very core of your church, and it will eliminate the tyranny, dangers, and risks of misalignment.

We call it *radical alignment,* and we believe it's been God's plan all along.

WHAT IS RADICAL ALIGNMENT?

Let's go back to our description of an Intentional Church—what it means to be One-aware, activated, and radically aligned.

> *The Intentional Church is concerned and well-informed about the lost, proactively keeping them top of mind. This knowledge and way of operating is so fundamental, far-reaching, and thorough that it becomes a key source of agreement and alliance in the church.*

It's right in there. Radical alignment is a fundamental, far-reaching, and thorough commitment to the Great Commission.

This alignment is radical because it's biblical, ancient, personal, and built to last.

The Bible tees it up well.
Let's start with the **mission**.

> *"For the Son of Man came to seek and save those who are lost."*
> —Luke 19:10

> *"Therefore, go and make disciples of all the nations, baptizing them in the name of the Father and the Son and the Holy Spirit. Teach these disciples to obey all the commands I have given you."*
> —Matthew 28:19–20

> *". . . there is more joy in heaven over one lost sinner who repents and returns to God than over ninety-nine others who are righteous and haven't strayed away!"*
> —Luke 15:7

> *"And God has given us this task of reconciling people to him. . . . And he gave us this wonderful message of reconciliation."*
> —2 Corinthians 5:18-19

The call for **alignment**.

> "Then make me truly happy by agreeing wholeheartedly with each other, loving one another, and working together with one mind and purpose."
> —Philippians 2:2

> "Make every effort to keep yourselves united in the Spirit, binding yourselves together with peace."
> —Ephesians 4:3

> "I appeal to you, dear brothers and sisters, by the authority of our Lord Jesus Christ, to live in harmony with each other. Let there be no divisions in the church. Rather, be of one mind, united in thought and purpose."
> —1 Corinthians 1:10

Now, God's **alignment model and method**.

> "Don't copy the behavior and customs of this world, but let God transform you into a new person by changing the way you think. Then you will learn to know God's will for you, which is good and pleasing and perfect."
> —Romans 12:2

> "Instead, let the Spirit renew your thoughts and attitudes."
> —Ephesians 4:23

> "And you must love the Lord your God with all your heart, all your soul, all your mind, and all your strength."
> —Mark 12:30

Finally, alignment. But to what end?
Activation!

> "But don't just listen to God's word. You must do what it says. Otherwise, you are only fooling yourselves."
> —James 1:22

> "What good is it, dear brothers and sisters, if you say you have faith but don't show it by your actions? Can that kind of faith save anyone?"
> —James 2:14

> "I know all the things you do, that you are neither hot nor cold. I wish that you were one or the other!"
> —Revelation 3:15

RADICAL ALIGNMENT GUIDED THE EARLY CHURCH

We owe these insights to Donald McGavran and Win Arn from their influential work *Ten Steps for Church Growth*.

The undeniable purpose of the church is to accomplish the Great Commission—to radically align mankind back to God through Christ. The early followers knew this from the get-go and took the directive seriously.

The directive began as early as Jesus's prayer at the Last Supper.

> *"Just as you sent me into the world,*
> *I am sending them into the world."*
>
> —John 17:18

His purpose was made clear throughout the prayer. Five times, Jesus emphasizes that *the world may believe*.

In His final earthly appearance to His disciples, Jesus gives this powerful prediction and directive.

> *You will receive power when the Holy Spirit comes upon you. And you will be my witnesses, telling people about me everywhere—in Jerusalem, throughout Judea, in Samaria, and to the ends of the earth.*
>
> —Acts 1:8

Wow! You must remember, his followers were sure that he came to restore the nation of Israel and establish an earthly kingdom. Instead, He turned the tables and sent them out to evangelize the world.

Expectations don't matter; His purpose does!

Then there are the instructions to us from Jesus himself. He told us to go and make disciples of all nations, baptizing and training them as we go. And most importantly, He promised to join us on the mission!

One note here about the Great Commission. Typically, *ta ethne* in the Greek from this passage is interpreted "all nations." We often think of this as the modern nation state—like the United States of America, India, China, Russia, and so on. A better interpretation is that we are called to bring every caste, tribe, tongue, people, and ethnic type on earth into a relationship with Jesus. That means anyone, anywhere, including those far and near to us.

It's clear how this impacted the early followers of Jesus. The extent of their world may have been limited compared to today, but this call still meant something significant. This is why Philip found himself ministering in Samaria. It wasn't a great distance physically, but it certainly was socially. He would have never gone there unless he knew it was the command of Jesus.

It's why Paul, who was more traveled and sophisticated, raised support, hiked, and got on boats to spread the Gospel in the Mediterranean area. Imagine Paul's epiphany about the call on both his life and the church as he met Jesus on the road to Damascus.

This once murderous, Jewish zealot wrote these telling passages.

> . . . *God chose me and called me by his marvelous grace. Then it pleased him to reveal his Son to me so that I would proclaim the Good News about Jesus to the Gentiles.*
>
> —Galatians 1:15–16

> *Through Christ, God has given us the privilege and authority as apostles to tell Gentiles everywhere what God has done for them, so that they will believe and obey him, bringing glory to his name.*
>
> —Romans 1:5

> *This message about Jesus Christ has revealed his plan for you Gentiles, a plan kept secret from the beginning of time. But now as the prophets foretold and as the eternal God has commanded, this message is made known to all Gentiles everywhere, so that they too might believe and obey him.*
>
> —Romans 16:25-26

The Great Commission was Paul's personal mission. Luke records it in Acts 20 as he is bidding farewell to the Ephesian church. Here it is, packed with radical alignment:

> *But my life is worth nothing to me unless I use it for finishing the work assigned me by the Lord Jesus—the work of telling others the Good News about the wonderful grace of God.*
>
> —Acts 20:24

The Great Commission is no random utterance of Jesus. It is marching orders for the church that still stands today—including your church.

God's eternal purpose is to reconcile mankind to Himself through the work of the Church. It has been His plan for 2,000 years and remains His plan today. Scripture gives testimony to this again and again.

A BIBLICAL CASE STUDY IN RADICAL ALIGNMENT

Paul's letter to the church in Philippi, written from a Roman prison, provides an incredible template for how a largely healthy church can align around the Great Commission. We often interpret the teaching in Philippians as having a very personal application. While this is true, Paul has a very strong message for the church, the body of Christ—a message about personal *and* organizational alignment to the mission.

Philippians is unique.

In his message, Paul includes the overseers and deacons right up front. Did you know this was the only time he addresses these leaders in the greeting of one of his letters?

> *I am writing to all of God's holy people in Philippi who belong to Christ Jesus, including the church leaders and deacons.*
>
> —Philippians 1:1

For the bulk of chapter 1, he sends a clear message that accomplishing the Great Commission requires a team effort. He makes it clear in verse 30 by saying, "We are in this struggle together."

Then, Paul challenges the Philippian leaders and believers to radically align around the gospel. It's a beautiful picture of striving alongside one another.

> *Above all, you must live as citizens of heaven, conducting yourselves in a manner worthy of the Good News about Christ. Then, whether I come and see you again or only hear about you, I will know that you are standing together with one spirit and one purpose, fighting together for the faith, which is the Good News.*
>
> —Philippians 1:27

Paul makes it clear that the source of alignment is the transformation of the heart that can only come from a relationship with Christ, having experienced His love. Your heart must first be broken for the mission in order for alignment to occur.

It's starting to sound radical, isn't it?

> *Is there any encouragement from belonging to Christ? Any comfort from his love? Any fellowship together in the Spirit? Are your hearts tender and compassionate? Then make me truly happy by agreeing wholeheartedly with each other, loving one another, and working together with one mind and purpose.*
>
> —Philippians 2:1–2

He speaks to God's alignment work within us, which sets us up to do what only God can do through us.

> *For God is working in you, giving you the desire and the power to do what pleases him.*
>
> —Philippians 2:13

In the Greek, it means God gives us the determination and the strength to radically align to the Great Commission.

Paul also makes it clear that there are enemies to radical alignment—pride and selfishness.

> *Don't be selfish; don't try to impress others. Be humble, thinking of others as better than yourselves. Don't look out only for your own interests, but take an interest in others, too.*
>
> —Philippians 2:3–4

And finally, in a great multidimensional way, Paul speaks to both the divine and personal partnership in church leadership.

> ... *for you have been my partners in spreading the Good News about Christ from the time you first heard it until now. And I am certain that God, who began the good work within you, will continue his work until it is finally finished on the day when Christ Jesus returns.*
>
> —Philippians 1:5–6

Often, this passage is only interpreted as having personal implications, but it is more profound than that. God is doing work in us to complete the mission together *through* us—spreading the Good News!

The Philippian case study helps us truly understand the purpose, power, and process of radical alignment. It's personal, and it's organizational.

And that's the essence of radical alignment—moving from *me* to *we* and from *my* transformation to *our* transformation! Remember, it's far-reaching and thorough.

We're going to get into the radical alignment process next. To fully understand it, you need to first understand the depth of its dimensions and the stages through which it occurs.

THE FIVE DIMENSIONS OF RADICAL ALIGNMENT

Radical alignment starts in you and then extends to your leadership team and church. Here's how we break it down.

Dimension #1: You Aligned with You

God has given us a model to follow in Scripture! It begins with the alignment of your heart (and soul), mind, and strength.

Heart — Your intentions, convictions, passions, and desires must first align with the mission of Jesus.

Mind — Now motivated, you must come to believe and understand the world as Jesus did. And thus, you come to think and reason as He did.

Strength — And finally, once you think and reason like Jesus, you can process, pursue, and set priorities as He did. You act as Jesus acted!

If there is a lack of alignment in *you*, there will be dissonance in your life that makes it nearly impossible to lead a radically aligned church. Your desires, understanding, and actions must first align with one another.

Do they?

What you desire must align with how you think. And how you think must align with how you are equipped and the actions you take.

Is this true in your life?

First, radical alignment requires a One-aware, activated, and aligned *you*.

Dimension #2: You Aligned with Your Leadership Team

The second dimension of radical alignment moves beyond your personal alignment. You must be aligned with each member of your leadership team.

Elders, staff, pastors, and lay leaders must share a similar heart, mind, and strength. This means you become mutually aligned in your core desires, understanding of the purposes of the church, and approach to church leadership.

Radical alignment requires a One-aware, activated, and aligned *leadership team*.

Dimension #3: You and Your Leadership Team Aligned with Your Congregation

The next dimension of radical alignment involves the congregation. You will not build a lasting One-aware and activated church without a significant number of believers who are willing to lead One-aware, activated, and radically aligned lives with you and your leadership team.

Radical alignment requires a One-aware, activated, and aligned *congregation*.

Dimension #4: Leadership Equipping Aligned to Leadership Roles

You, and every other leader in your church, are a part of the Ninety-Nine. Everyone in your church is called to align their heart, mind, and strength, including you. By personally aligning to the Great Commission, you are aligning to one another.

There is another dimension. As a leader, you have a unique role to play in the church, which means there is an additional aspect to your alignment. This is the fourth dimension of radical alignment—the equipping of the heart, mind, and strength required for your unique role in leadership.

The unique roles in leadership include:

- Elders/Overseers (Board)
- Pastors and Staff
- Lay Leadership

Radical alignment requires unique One-aware, activated, and aligned *leadership equipping*.

Dimension #5: Church Resources Aligned to the Great Commission

The fifth and final dimension is the resulting alignment of your church's time and resources toward reaching the One. To achieve One-awareness and activation, you must apply a One-aware lens to every decision you make as a leadership team.

This dimension of radical alignment will happen naturally as you align the hearts, minds, and strength of every believer and leader in your congregation. It's the final test of radical alignment and an outcome of the other dimensions being in alignment. If your resources are not aligned to the Great Commission, then you are probably misaligned in one or more of the other dimensions.

Radical alignment requires One-aware, activated, and aligned *church resources.*

Are your church's time and resources dedicated to mobilizing the Ninety-Nine to reaching the One?

Paul was right! Radical alignment is multidimensional.

Let's pause for a quick check-in.

Right now, you might be thinking, *There's a lot to this alignment thing. Where in the world do I start?* Don't worry. We have built a powerful tool to help you know where to start, point out gaps, and understand what to do next.

> **Radical alignment requires One-aware, activated, and aligned *church resources.***

For now, hang in there! There are also stages to the process of radical alignment. It isn't going to happen overnight.

THE THREE STAGES OF RADICAL ALIGNMENT

These are the stages of alignment we've identified. It won't happen all at once.

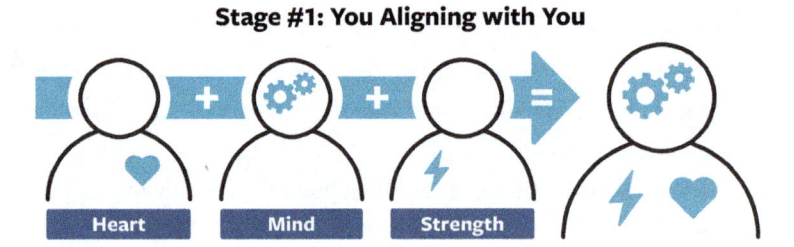

Stage #1: You Aligning with You

Heart | Mind | Strength

Stage #2: You Aligning with Your Leadership Team (Pastors, Staff, and Board)

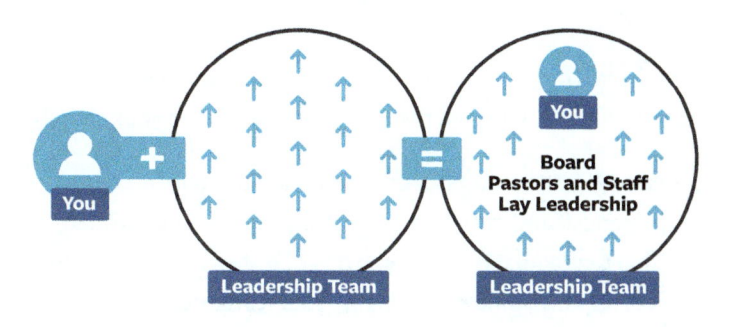

[Diagram: You + Leadership Team = Leadership Team (Board, Pastors and Staff, Lay Leadership) with You]

Stage #3: Your Leadership Team (You, Pastors, Staff, and Board) Aligning with Your Congregation

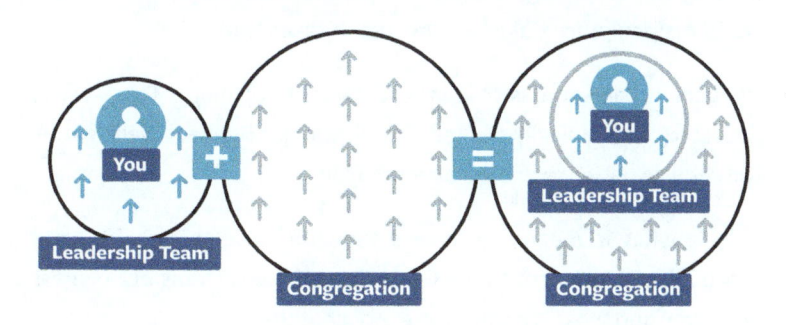

[Diagram: You with Leadership Team + Congregation = Congregation with You and Leadership Team]

RADICAL ALIGNMENT REQUIRES PATIENCE

Don't copy the behavior and customs of this world, but let God transform you into a new person by changing the way you think. Then you will learn to know God's will for you, which is good and pleasing and perfect.

—Romans 12:2

As we described earlier, radical alignment to the Great Commission is a spiritual matter requiring transformation of the heart, mind, and strength.

Don't miss it. The Great Commission must become a personal mission statement first for you, and then for every believer in your church.

You must learn how to be a good steward of your life and ensure One-awareness and activation are always top of mind. Then, your leadership team must learn how to be good stewards of the church's resources to this same end. Finally, your congregation must learn how to live this way and be contributing members of a body fully committed to the Great Commission.

Spiritual growth experts tell us that it could take years for a new believer to completely reorient their life to the lordship of Christ. It could happen more quickly, but often, it takes time.

We believe the same is true in leadership. Becoming a One-aware, activated, and radically aligned church will not happen overnight. It will require patience and persistent effort.

This is what it means to have a fundamental, far-reaching, and thorough commitment to the Great Commission. This is our biggest discovery and what we want for every church.

One church, on one mission. For generations.

Churches in our movement are experiencing this radical alignment. It's not a quick fix or silver bullet, but it's a journey you can begin today.

For Individual Reflection and Application:

1. Review the symptoms of misalignment. Which ones do you recognize in your personal leadership or church experience?

2. Do you see misalignment in any of the five dimensions? How does this impact you personally?

3. Consider the three stages of radical alignment. Which stage best describes where you are currently, and what would moving to the next stage require?

For Team Discussion and Interaction:

1. Look at the four church types (Wobbly, Stalemate, Retreating, Advancing). Which best describes your church currently, and what would it take to become truly aligned?

2. Discuss the statement: "Radical alignment requires moving from 'me' to 'we' and from 'my' transformation to 'our' transformation." What would this look like practically in your leadership team? Church?

AN INTENTIONAL CHURCH STORY

From Consumer Christianity to Great Commission Living: How Pathway Church Achieved Radical Alignment

Pathway Church in south-central Kansas discovered that true growth requires more than good intentions—it demands radical alignment to the Great Commission at every level of the organization. Executive Pastor Rodney Elliott shares their four-year journey of transformation that led to over 500 baptisms in three years.

The Challenge of Consumer Christianity
Elliott identifies a core problem plaguing many churches: members who have grown comfortable consuming church services rather than living out Jesus' mission. "For those who have grown up in church, it can be easy to get stuck in a consumer mindset," he explains. "They've never really been a part of the Great Commission. They've never lived out the mission of Jesus, instead consuming things that the church provides and thinking it's the finish line."

Starting with Leadership
The transformation began with their elder board using the Intentional Church model for strategic alignment. Elliott emphasizes that board meetings couldn't remain business-focused but had to become personal journeys of living out the Great Commission. "The people who are generally on most church boards have been Christians the longest and are the most insulated," he notes. "Sometimes, it takes even longer than with your congregation to help them change their mindset."

Redefining Evangelism
Pathway Church reframed evangelism from intimidating confrontations to simple friendship. "You don't have to be an evangelist to love people, to be there for them, and to show them who Jesus is," Elliott shares. "The job is not the institutional church's job. The job is yours." They celebrate ordinary acts of kindness—meeting neighbors,

bringing meals, being present—as vital components of the Great Commission.

The Cost and Reward
This shift wasn't without opposition. Elliott acknowledges that focusing on reaching the lost can be polarizing within the church. Some argued they shouldn't reach so many people if they couldn't properly disciple them. His response: "We are the discipleship plan."

The result? A church where "a couple thousand people would find one person who doesn't know Jesus, be a good friend, legitimately care about them, pray, and see what God does." Elliott believes this simple approach, multiplied across the congregation, could unleash "an amazing movement."

Elliott's story offers hope for pastors struggling with stagnant growth and consumer-minded congregations. True transformation requires patience, intentionality, and the courage to make comfortable Christians uncomfortable. It starts with leadership alignment and extends through every layer of the church until the Great Commission becomes not just a mission statement but a way of life for every member.

Read Pathway's Full Story Here

CHAPTER 5

7 Steps to Jump-Start the Journey

We've come a long way.

We made a case for radical alignment by looking at the discoveries from our first dozen years and work with 1,000 churches. We've been open about our experiences and challenges.

We looked at the biblical truths about alignment to the Great Commission and cast a vision for the power of a new (old) solution called *radical alignment*. We've explained why it is indeed radical.

Some of these insights may be a revelation for you. Much of what we've shared is likely a confirmation of things you've noticed for years.

In the end, we've been challenging you to think seriously about aligning your life, leadership, and church radically to the Great Commission and becoming a truly Intentional Church.

What's next?

In our experience, conviction starts with awareness, then proceeds to a holy discontentment, and eventually becomes a firm resolve to change. You know you're ready for a change when the pain of staying the same, or the potential gains of living differently, outweigh the costs of the changes required to alleviate the pain or realize the gains.

Are you there? We know you're ready!

What follows is exactly how we would begin the journey if we were in your shoes. We are going to share some tools from the Intentional Churches Toolbox. We'll also give you some instructions and tips for using the tools later.

What is a church leadership tool? A tool is a biblically based framework through which you, your team, and your congregation can process information with the guidance of the Holy Spirit. It supports a strategic conversation for the purposes of One-awareness, activation, and alignment to the Great Commission.

SEVEN STEPS TO JUMP-START THE JOURNEY

1. Determine the Destination
2. Trust Your Team
3. Assess Honestly
4. Embrace the Tension
5. Narrow the Focus
6. Organize for Action
7. Pray with Purpose

STEP 1

Determine the Destination

Then make me truly happy by agreeing wholeheartedly with each other, loving one another, and working together with one mind and purpose.

—Philippians 2:2

Everyone needs a similar vision of an Intentional Church as you begin the journey.

A Vision of Radical Alignment. What does a One-aware, activated, and radically aligned church look like? Here are some simple descriptions that will help.

A vision of the Intentional Church . . .

- Every leader and many, if not all, of the Ninety-Nine have identified and built at least one genuine relationship with a non-believer from their relational reach zone for the purpose of intentional and prayerful spiritual influence.

- Elders, pastors, staff, and lay leadership understand their roles clearly and process decisions through a unified, One-aware mindset and rationale. They also model a One-aware and activated lifestyle for the congregation.

- Weekend services, discipleship opportunities, and all church programs and ministries have a One-aware filter, or set of lenses, through which they are seen. Reaching the One is thought of first and often in all activities. The One is never forgotten.

- Conversions are happening regularly as a result of a mobilized and trained Ninety-Nine in relationship with their Ones. There are safe spaces for the spiritually searching to find answers to their questions.

- There are clear definitions for terms, a common language is used, and there are consistent standards for evaluation. The church's calendar, budget, and resources are aligned to the Great Commission. Vision is clear, priorities are clarified, and there's a high sense of accountability to follow through on the plans God has given.

That's a lot to chew on. Take a minute. It's not going to happen overnight, but you can't start the journey if you don't know the visionary destination.

You must begin by level-setting so no one defines the goal for themselves! Now that you have a clear picture of radical alignment, let's go to the next step.

STEP 2
Trust your Team

So don't go to war without wise guidance;
victory depends on having many advisers.

—Proverbs 24:6

You are about to embark on a counterintuitive journey, one that begins with an honest evaluation of your current situation and requires trust in your team and the process. It will ultimately require trust in the Holy Spirit to lead you forward.

Don't begin this journey alone! Put a team together and trust that the answers are in your team and the Holy Spirit will help you find them.

> **Tip:** Put a team together with differing perspectives. Consider people with fresh eyes, a long history with you and your church, unique roles, or a deep concern for aligning to the Great Commission and reaching the lost. We can't overstate the value of seeking insight and direction from multiple perspectives.

Don't forget your most important team member!

> *And I will ask the Father, and he will give you another Advocate, who will never leave you. He is the Holy Spirit, who leads into all truth. The world cannot receive him, because it isn't looking for him and doesn't recognize him. But you know him, because he lives with you now and later will be in you.*
>
> —John 14:16–17

STEP 3
Assess Honestly

Then the Lord God called to the man, "Where are you?"

—Genesis 3:9

Radical alignment always begins with and requires accurate and honest evaluation. It has been God's way from the beginning.

But don't take our word for it.

In Romans, as Paul speaks of the renewing of our minds, he follows with the beginning place—the headwaters of renewal:

> *I give each of you this warning: Don't think you are better than you really are. Be honest in your evaluation of yourselves, measuring yourselves by the faith God has given us.*
>
> —Romans 12:3

Why? Maybe it's because we can be too close, or be too proud, or just move too fast. Or maybe it's because the enemy uses what's left in the hidden spaces to undermine plans for alignment to God's mission. Regardless, it's important to start your search with honest assessment.

It might be counterintuitive, but truth, even unpleasant truth, is your friend. These are the simple questions to ask in the beginning.

- Where are we today? *Really.*
- How did we get here? *Honestly.*

That's why the Intentional Churches Toolbox is loaded with proven ways to assess your situation with sound judgment.

We're going to unpack the "hunting for truth" techniques we teach because this step is so important. We believe that 50 percent of making a plan is finding the truth and seeing it for what it is. Take your time.

When you begin with an honest hunt for the truth, you will find it's easier to determine a vision for the future, and the action in front of you should naturally emerge. It takes discipline and courage but will be so rewarding.

Make Notes. You are going to harvest the Holy Spirit's insights through a discussion. You can do this by making notes as you go, or you can gather thoughts after your discussion. If you wait until the end, have your team make notes about their thoughts as you go so no Holy Spirit insight is left behind.

Frame and Focus Your Search. It's really helpful to have a model or framework to guide you and your discussions in your hunt for truth. This helps everyone process thoughts together as you begin your journey.

Framework #1: The Four Commodities

We teach every church about the Four Commodities of Life and Leadership. Everyone has them available. Each of us uses them. They are the means by which we live and lead.

The Four Commodities of Life and Leadership

| Time | Money | Energy | Attention |

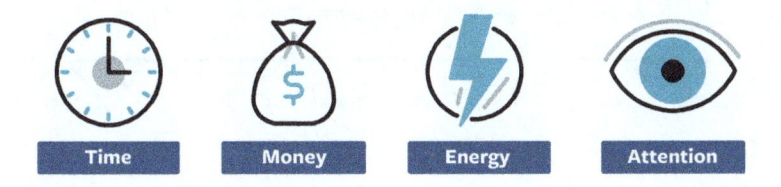

We all have these because God has given them to us. What you do with them means everything to the radical alignment of your life, leadership team, and church. This is the essence of good stewardship.

By taking a close look at these commodities, you can begin to see the truth when it comes to radical alignment. The evidence is found through an honest audit driven by the power of questions.

It's as simple as this. How much of each commodity is intentionally focused on your One(s)? Here are some quick check-ins to gauge your awareness and activation when it comes to your personal commitment to the Great Commission. Take a minute. Think about it. Be honest!

YOUR CALENDAR (TIME)
How much of my calendar is One-aware and activated?

0% — 50% — 100%

YOUR BANK ACCOUNT AND BUDGET (MONEY)
How much of my resources are One-aware and activated?

0% — 50% — 100%

YOUR EFFORT, SKILLS, AND TALENTS (ENERGY)
How often are my skills and talents One-aware and activated?

Never — Sometimes — Often

YOUR THOUGHTS AND FOCUS (ATTENTION)
How often is my mind One-aware and activated?

Never — Sometimes — Often

Does that make sense? Simple, huh.

However, alignment is interconnected. Just as you have a finite amount of time, money, energy, and attention, the same is true for each member of your team as well as your church. It involves everyone.

Questions Help the Hunt. Learn the art of asking questions. Questions are powerful! When you read or hear a statement, you might simply process and store it, but a question engages the brain in a much deeper way.

Here are some more questions for your hunt. Start with personal reflection and then discuss these with your team.

- Am I aligned in my heart, mind, and strength with the Great Commission as one of the Ninety-Nine in my church? Are my pastors, staff, and lay leaders personally aligned? Is the rest of the Ninety-Nine?

- Is our leadership team aligned in heart? Are they aligned with a passion and call to lead a One-aware, activated, and radically aligned church? What about each of us as leaders? And when it comes to our mind and strength, are we really equipped to lead a radically aligned church?

> **Tip:** Allow the conversation to flow from various perspectives. God gives insights to each person from their own experiences and backgrounds and guides your team. Also, don't try to solve problems as you go. This is honest discovery. It might create tension, but that's okay. Remember, that tension is going to guide you and push you forward.

Framework #2: Radical Alignment Ratings

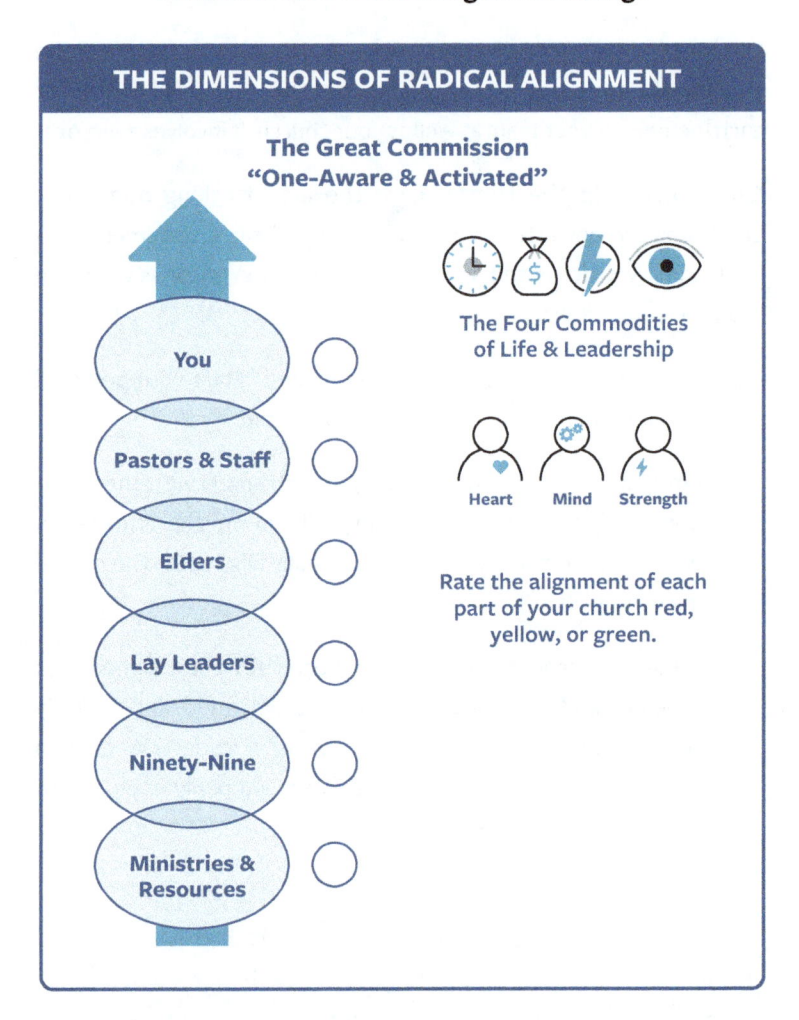

THE DIMENSIONS OF RADICAL ALIGNMENT

The Great Commission
"One-Aware & Activated"

- You
- Pastors & Staff
- Elders
- Lay Leaders
- Ninety-Nine
- Ministries & Resources

The Four Commodities of Life & Leadership

Heart   Mind   Strength

Rate the alignment of each part of your church red, yellow, or green.

A red/yellow/green rating method is another great way to drive discussion and find the truth. The circles to the right of the dimensions of the following tool can be used for this exercise. Simply ask each team member to give a radical alignment rating to each dimension and make notes about their reasoning using the definitions of each color.

Red/Yellow/Green Rating:

- Red = Not One-aware, activated, or aligned to the Great Commission

- Yellow = Somewhat One-aware, activated, and aligned to the Great Commission but room for improvement

- Green = One-aware, activated, and aligned to the Great Commission; effective and healthy

Discuss why each team member gave the ratings they did. What was God revealing to them? Where is there misalignment? What is causing it? Where is there alignment?

You will be amazed at the different perspectives and insights from each team member. Don't be caught off guard, and don't jump to solutions just yet.

Harvesting Insights with Four Helpful Lists

After working through these frameworks, harvest your thoughts and honest assessments with the Four Helpful Lists tool. It is built on the power of four simple but powerful questions. With your thorough discussion in mind, ask: What is *right* that we can build upon? What is *wrong* that must be fixed? What is *missing* that must be added? What is *confused* that must be clarified?

Honest, real evaluation should be your starting point for all attempts at becoming One-aware, activated, and radically aligned

FOUR HELPFUL LISTS	
RIGHT? (Amplify)	**WRONG?** (Fix)
<ul><li>_____</li><li>_____</li><li>_____</li><li>_____</li><li>_____</li><li>_____</li></ul>	<ul><li>_____</li><li>_____</li><li>_____</li><li>_____</li><li>_____</li><li>_____</li></ul>
MISSING? (Add)	**CONFUSED?** (Clarify)
<ul><li>_____</li><li>_____</li><li>_____</li><li>_____</li><li>_____</li><li>_____</li></ul>	<ul><li>_____</li><li>_____</li><li>_____</li><li>_____</li><li>_____</li><li>_____</li></ul>

Used by permission from the Paterson Center

Honest, real evaluation should be your starting point for all attempts at becoming One-aware, activated, and radically aligned. This is what we mean by hunting for the truth. And remember, the Devil will use even the slightest bit of dishonesty to gain a foothold in your ministry.

> **Tip:** You are using Intentional Growth Planning whether you realized it or not! It's the core processor of the Intentional Churches Toolbox. Right now, you are not only beginning the journey to radical alignment, but you are also learning how to use the toolbox to get there!

Time for the next step.

STEP 4
Embrace the Tension

> *And I am certain that God, who began the good work within you, will continue his work until it is finally finished on the day when Christ Jesus returns.*
>
> —Philippians 1:6

As Christians, we live in the in-between—the now, already, and not yet. There is a natural tension that is created when we live out, and lead through, God's plan for radical alignment.

This tension is a powerful, positive, and useful force. We told you we would show you how it helps. There are two ways to set the tension in a healthy way.

The Truth. When you use biblical tools to honestly evaluate where you stand, it can get uncomfortable and tense. It can even be personally challenging and discouraging, but God is going to use this to motivate and create a foundation for progress. He will honor your honesty and provide direction.

We know this will cause pressure to arise within you and your team. Great pressure can be used to power progress just like it powers a massive locomotive. When done with the right heart, for the right purpose, and with good processes, it will propel your church forward.

> **Tip:** Remind yourself often that we only grade, rate, and assess things as a hunt for Holy Spirit–driven insight and action. If He gives us insight that is going to lead to the right next steps to take, He will also give us comfort as things get tense. And never weaponize the comments and conversation!

It's now time to add the tension of vision to the mix.

The Vision. When you frame your future clearly and compellingly, you are going to see the gap between today's reality and the possibilities of tomorrow. This will create more tension. But again, God is going to use this to motivate you and pull you forward. Your priorities are naturally going to emerge.

First, set a time frame. The time horizon is so important when setting a vision or even goals. You need to live in the future for a few minutes, envisioning what's possible when it comes to radical alignment. Our recommendation for this exercise is to start with a one-year time frame.

Next, let your questions be your friend. Pray, step mentally into the future, and ask the following questions of yourself and your team—making notes as you go.

- In one year, where am I when it comes to the radical alignment of my mind, heart, and strength to the Great Commission? What does my life look like when it comes to how I use my time, energy, money, and attention?

Leadership Team Questions:

- In one year, where are we when it comes to the radical alignment of our team's minds, hearts, and strength to the Great Commission? What does our life as a team look like when it comes to how we use our time, energy, money, and attention?

- In one year, how do the lives of our Ninety-Nine look when it comes to the radical alignment of their minds, hearts, and strength to the Great Commission? What do their lives as followers look like when it comes to how they use their time, energy, money, and attention?

- In one year, how does our church look when it comes to the radical alignment of our collective minds, hearts, and strength to the Great Commission? What does it look like in how our church uses its time, energy, money, and attention?

Can you see it? Do you feel it? Do you want it?

Good vision is concrete, clear, and compelling. Vision can be a combination of qualitative and quantitative statements—meaning it can be an emphatic future statement, or it can include numbers. But it must always be clear enough to be seen, realistic enough to be believed, big enough to stretch and inform your next steps, and inspiring enough to provide the motivation and strength to give it your all.

Visioning is often seen as some mystical exercise. We think it's as simple as knowing where you stand, choosing the right horizon, and asking very clear future questions set against a solid biblical framework.

Emotions. Vision, along with honest evaluations, can stir up emotions. We've seen leaders pound their fists and be completely broken down by the hunt for truth. We've also seen leaders be equally as anxious about defining a preferred future in the name of the Great Commission. It's both an aspirational exercise and a practical one in our view, and always the result of the Holy Spirit's direction.

> **Tip:** Visioning is a muscle you and your team will develop in time. Don't sweat it too much the first few times through. God will give you the visions He wants you to see for now. Remember, you learn as you repeat this leadership cycle again and again, and you will grow in your ability. Eventually, it will become intuitive and second nature.

The tension of truth and vision directs us. It pushes us forward. It pulls us together. Let's embrace it. (And maybe even try to create it occasionally!)

STEP 5
Narrow the Focus

So I run with purpose in every step.
I am not just shadowboxing.

—1 Corinthians 9:26

If you have followed our direction with discipline, you should have a clear sense of where you stand as a follower, leader, and church. You should also have clarity, given by the Holy Spirit, about what's possible and where God wants you to be in the near future.

The tension between truth and vision helps to clarify next steps. The gap in between contains the work to move you forward. Your job is to define and align your work, prioritize it, and unlock your potential. You and your church have amazing potential because of the Holy Spirit and the Gospel. It's time to let it loose!

Make a List. Here is a simple tool that can help you spot the items in the gap between today and tomorrow.

STRATEGIC ACTION LONG LIST	
VIP'S	**LOW HANGING FRUIT**
• _____ • _____ • _____ • _____ • _____ • _____	• _____ • _____ • _____ • _____ • _____ • _____
PAUSE?	**STOP?**
• _____ • _____ • _____ • _____ • _____ • _____	• _____ • _____ • _____ • _____ • _____ • _____

- **VIP (Vision Initiative Project).** What feels like it's a big enough set of tasks to require a team? You will probably have some projects that you see in your year ahead.

- **Low-Hanging Fruit.** What can be easily accomplished? You will likely see some more simple things you can do that will give you quick wins.

- **Pause?** Is God leading you to put anything on pause? For instance, you may be planning to spend money on something that can be delayed until you assess its purpose for better alignment to the Great Commission.

- **Stop?** Is God leading you to stop something altogether? You may see that a regular activity or ministry program is pulling the Ninety-Nine away from a focus on the One.

After completing this exercise, a long list of possible action items may emerge. Often, it all seems important. Here are some crucial next steps.

Sort Your Work. The items on your list will likely range in scope, depth, and breadth—from big and complex to small and simple. Sort the big from the small and get ready to hand out some of the smaller items as assignments. Pluck some of the low-hanging fruit quickly if you can!

Prioritize and Sequence. For the bigger, more involved projects, your job as a team is to agree on the priority and sequencing of your work. What should happen first, and what should happen next?

Here's a powerful question that can help you: If you could only tackle one of these items at a time, which would come first, next, and so on? Force yourself to think narrowly. It's good stewardship to think this way.

One at a Time. You may be ready to go but tempted to tackle a lot of the items at once. We've seen it again and again—and the price that is paid when too much is attempted at the same time.

If you want to release the gospel potential in your church and move toward radical alignment, line your projects up one at a time and knock them out in order.

You've probably heard the axiom: We often overestimate what we can do in the short term and underestimate what can be accomplished in the long run if we work with focus and discipline. This is definitely true in church leadership. Be disciplined, and you'll be amazed how far you can move toward radical alignment in just one year.

Another quick check-in. We are compressing a process we know works into a few pages. We know it will work, and we've done it 1,000 times—literally. Don't feel like you have to go through all seven steps in one fell swoop. It's okay to take your time and walk through the steps over a few sessions. Patience will serve you well, especially your first time through. And always remember, we and our community are here to help!

STEP 6
Organize for Action

We can make our plans,
but the Lord determines our steps.

—Proverbs 16:9

There's wisdom in doing this process with others.

Remember when Moses was overwhelmed with the complexity of leading the children of Israel? Jethro, his concerned father-in-law, asked him a few simple questions: "What are you trying to accomplish here?" and "Why are you trying to do this alone while everyone stands around you from morning till evening?" Yikes!

We've all fallen into the lonely leader trap. Let's be clear about what we're trying to do, and let's get others around us to help.

Form a Cross-Functional VIP Team. We are big believers in putting a diverse group of leaders together to execute the work God has put in front of you. In an earlier tip, we recommended you put a team together with differing perspectives. The same is true here in the formation of a VIP (Vision Initiative Project) team.

Pulling together a few people from various backgrounds, skills, and passions to work on a project can have a profound impact. VIPs are an opportunity to develop leaders, create ownership, and elevate your team's thinking. They are unifying and directly connected to accomplishing your vision with God's help.

> We've all fallen into the lonely leader trap. Let's be clear about what we're trying to do, and let's get others around us to help.

Clarity Is Kindness. Be clear about the purpose of the project, who is in charge of it, who is on the team, and what action will be taken.

- Objective. *What are we setting out to do?* Write a one- or two-sentence statement that clarifies the purpose of the project.

- Ownership. *Who is leading this project?* Be sure everyone is clear on who is responsible for the objective and who is on the team to help.

- Action Plan. *What steps do we need to take?* Outline who is doing what and by when.

Here is a simple but effective action planning tool you can use to create ongoing clarity and accountability:

IMMEDIATE ACTION PLAN		
ITEM	OWNER	DUE DATE

Begin to knock out your action steps, and remember to celebrate as God brings progress and victories. He will do so because of your honesty, courage, and discipline!

> **Tip:** Name an Activator. This is a key role that involves stewardship and service but is focused on accountability. The Activator has permission to keep you and your team accountable to your commitments and to moving forward over time. He or she asks questions like: *Who's doing what by when? What have you accomplished? Where are you stuck? When are we meeting again? What do we need to celebrate?* You need an Intentional Churches trained Activator!

Discipline. Radical alignment requires discipline and won't come easily at first. It's rigorous at times, even uncomfortable. It involves introspection and, sometimes, difficult conversations. But there is a great reward coming.

Again, don't take our word for it.

> *No discipline is enjoyable while it is happening—it's painful! But afterward there will be a peaceful harvest of right living for those who are trained in this way. So take a new grip with your tired hands and strengthen your weak knees. Mark out a straight path for your feet so that those who are weak and lame will not fall but become strong.*
>
> —Hebrews 12:11–13

STEP 7
Pray with Purpose

And we are confident that he hears us whenever we ask for anything that pleases him.

—1 John 5:14

Your final step is *prayer*—a proactive, organized plan for prayer. Do you have a plan to release the power of the Holy Spirit through prayer and hear from Him as you go?

You probably need no reminder, but here's why this matters:

Power. It's going to take power to achieve radical alignment. The dynamic power of the Holy Spirit is released through prayer. The Holy Spirit does many things in and for us. We receive comfort, wisdom, and insight when we pray. Our conviction and confidence grow. You will never experience sustained radical alignment to the Great Commission without the power of the Holy Spirit.

Protection. Your enemy is roaming around, seeking those he can devour. He wants none of this alignment to happen. Leading a dynamic, change-oriented, moving, living, and breathing church presents many opportunities for the Devil to gain a foothold. Create a proactive plan for prayer to protect you, your leadership, and your congregation. Design it, communicate about it, and get lots of people to do it with you.

Peace. Fear is the number one challenge for most church leaders. It manifests from many places—fear of confrontation, lack of resources, and losing people we love as we push through the changes required to fully align to the Great Commission. This lack of peace can stymie your progress. God has gone before us in all of this; He will go beside us and even after us in the wake of our mistakes. We are reminded of this as we pray and lay our plans before Him.

Make It Real. Oh yeah. This isn't real until it's in your calendar. You don't have a proactive plan for prayer until you know who's doing it and when. We had one church determine they weren't embarking on the journey until they had put together a twenty-four-hour prayer team to pray for a month in advance. We think that's a good idea for all of us.

We've added a prayer component to the Great Commission Engine Tool used in the Intentional Churches Toolbox. In our view, it's the fuel and the insurance policy for the whole model. That's pretty accurate. Proactive prayer must be a priority ingredient for an Intentional Church.

We promise you are about to see things move. Radical alignment is underway. Again, it's not because of you or anything we've helped you to understand. It's because radical alignment to the Great Commission is what God wants.

It's not our idea; it's His.

It's not because of our desire or strength; it's because of His.

The planting and watering are ours to do, but the fruit of alignment is His to produce.

For Individual Reflection and Application:

1. To what degree would you say you are personally committed—One-aware and activated—in each of the four commodities (time, money, energy, and attention)? How could you grow your commitment in that area?

2. Work through the Four Helpful Lists tool for your personal leadership: What's right, wrong, missing, and confused in your current approach?

3. Develop a personal proactive prayer plan. How will you specifically pray for protection, power, and peace as you pursue radical alignment?

For Team Discussion and Interaction:

1. Complete the Red/Yellow/Green rating exercise together for each dimension of radical alignment. Compare your assessments and discuss the differences.

2. Use the custom Four Box Action Tool to identify your VIP Projects, Low-Hanging Fruit, items to Pause, and items to Stop. Prioritize and sequence your work together.

3. Work all of the seven steps together as a team!

AN INTENTIONAL CHURCH STORY

Radical Alignment: How Journey Church Found Their Voice in Reaching the Lost

Journey Church in Jackson, Tennessee, proves that radical alignment isn't just a buzzword—it's the key to explosive Kingdom growth. What started as 40 committed believers has exploded to 850 members in fifteen years, all while maintaining laser focus on their original mission: the Great Commission.

The Challenge of Church Plant Alignment

Lead Pastor Jeremy Brown and Teaching Pastor Kris Pace discovered that even church plants aren't immune to mission drift. Despite launching with sold-out believers, they faced the typical struggle of transitioning "small-church mindsets" to think "outsiders first, us second." As Jeremy puts it, "Alignment is not something you're going to come by simply—even in a church plant. It's something you have to fight tooth and nail for, in every conversation."

The Power of Common Language

Four years ago, Journey partnered with Intentional Churches, not because they lacked focus, but because they wanted radical alignment in their language across all ministries. The result? Everyone from elder board to volunteers now speaks the same language when discussing their 70/30 focus—reaching the lost while caring for the found.

Kris discovered Journey's DNA through fifty conversations with members, hearing virtually the same response: "Journey may be the best place for somebody who doesn't know Jesus to come and know Jesus." This culture of acceptance—where neck tattoos and rough backgrounds are celebrated rather than judged—creates the perfect environment for transformation.

Transformation in Action

The Vision Initiative Project teams showcase this alignment's power. Ben, initially dragged to church by his wife, became an impact player after understanding Journey's "One" focus. Now he leads Bible discussions at home and helps reach other Ones—proving that clear alignment transforms consumers into missionaries.

The Bottom Line

Journey's success stems from fighting relentlessly for alignment around Scripture-based strategy. They're on track to double their impact ahead of schedule, implementing the model deeply and preparing for a $5 million building campaign. Their secret? Radical alignment that turns every member into a Great Commission warrior, proving that when churches align around reaching the lost, growth follows naturally.

Read Journey's Full Story Here

CHAPTER 6

3 Ways to Not Get Stuck

It's not by accident that our paths crossed.

God is patiently and persistently trying to get our attention, to align us with Him. We believe it's the desire of His heart for us personally and also for our churches.

You have started the journey toward radical alignment. Now it's time to accelerate it and make sure you don't get stuck.

ASSESS > ADVANCE > ABIDE

ASSESS

> Jesus said to the people who believed in him, "You are truly my disciples if you remain faithful to my teachings. And you will know the truth, and the truth will set you free."
>
> —John 8:31–32

> **You have started the journey toward radical alignment. Now it's time to accelerate it and make sure you don't get stuck.**

Again, we'll repeat the importance of beginning the journey to radical alignment with honest assessment. It's not only the place to start; it's the place to come back to again and again.

We've helped countless churches learn the process of Intentional Growth Planning—the core processor of the Intentional Churches Toolbox. It helps to organize the toolbox and represents a cycle you can use to become and stay radically aligned to the Great Commission.

INTENTIONAL GROWTH PLANNING

The Spiritual Battlefield

- Your Team
- Today's Battle
- Tomorrow's Challenges
- Chasm To Cross/ Bridge to Build
- Hill To Take
- Future Vision

1. DISCOVER
- Today's Truth
- Our Journey

2. DESIGN
- The One
- Engagement
- Double Vision

Center: The One / The Great Commission / Double Kingdom Impact

3. ORGANIZE
- Dashboard
- VIPs
- Immediate Action

4. ACTIVATE
- Rhythms
- Meetings
- Reports

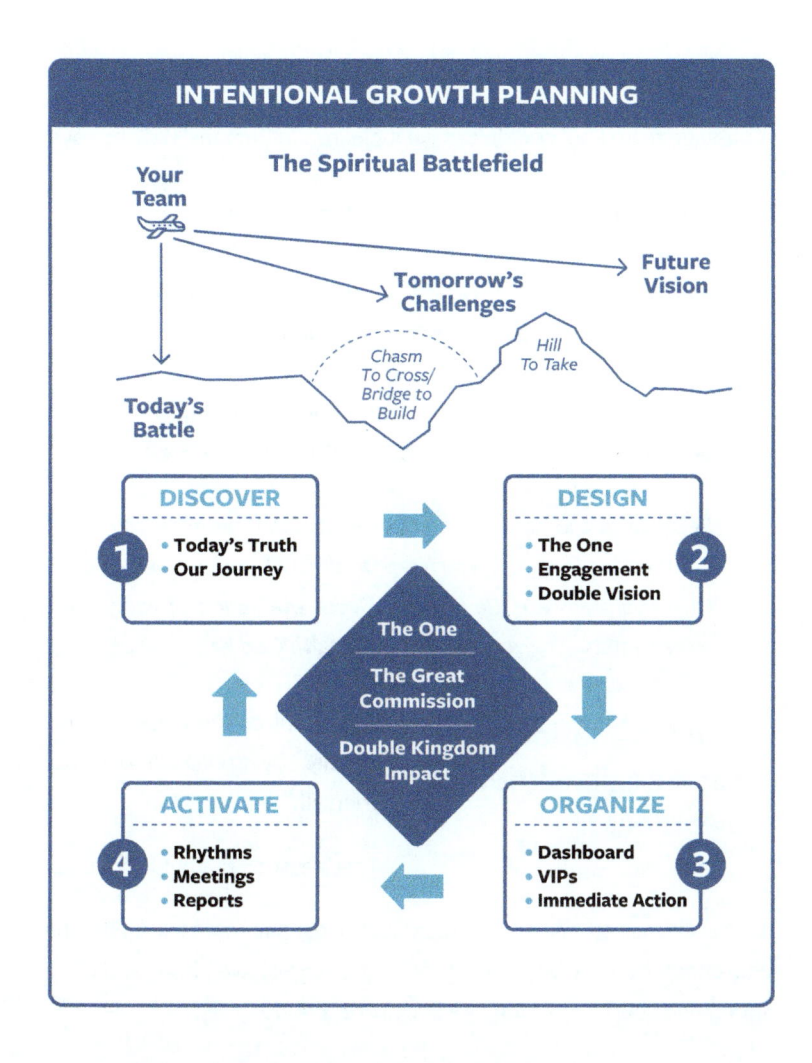

- Step 1 - Discovery: *Where are we today?*
- Step 2 - Design: *Where is God calling us to go?*
- Step 3 - Organize: *What are our priorities?*
- Step 4 - Activate: *How will we be accountable?*

You experienced Intentional Growth Planning in the last chapter. In every case, no matter how often or how many times you repeat the process, it starts with an assessment.

Why? Transformation can't begin without awareness.

A passage from Paul couldn't make it clearer. In Romans 12:2, he says:

> *Don't copy the behavior and customs of this world, but let God transform you into a new person by changing the way you think. Then you will learn to know God's will for you, which is good and pleasing and perfect.*

Then, in the very next verse, he delivers a stern warning and offers a defense of why transformation begins with honest assessment.

> *Because of the privilege and authority God has given me, I give each of you this warning: Don't think you are better than you really are. Be honest in your evaluation of yourselves, measuring yourselves by the faith God has given us.*

> **Transformation can't begin without awareness.**

If you look at the Greek, Paul is literally saying, "Don't overrate yourself."

That's easy to say, but hard to do.

It's never easy to honestly assess ourselves, our ministries, and the churches where we've labored for years. We all have biases and blind spots, and there's nothing like Scripture to help.

The Radical Alignment Assessment™

What Is It? The Radical Alignment Assessment™ gives you the opportunity to compare yourself, your team, and your church to God's word. Scripture is our benchmark, our measuring stick, and the lens through which we examine ourselves. In the assessment, we'll cover all the aspects of radical alignment we've discussed in this book.

- The alignment of *your* heart, mind, and actions to the Great Commission

  You

- The alignment of *your team's* hearts, minds, and actions to the Great Commission

  Leadership Team

- The alignment of *your congregation's* hearts, minds, and actions to the Great Commission

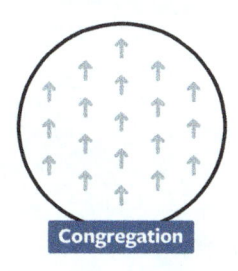

  Congregation

How Does It Work? The assessment is a guided conversation between you and God, using Scripture. That way, you're not the only one doing the evaluation; you're allowing the "alive and powerful" Word of God and the Holy Spirit to reveal your "innermost thoughts and desires" (Hebrews 4:12). It's designed to be completed by you and by members of your leadership team. That way, we can provide both individual and team results.

How Does It Help? You'll gain a fresh perspective, discover your gaps, and identify specific areas of focus. It will naturally create the tension that leads to action. Again, this is so important because awareness precedes conviction and is the first step in transformation. The assessment is a baseline, a starting point for your journey.

However, we have a concern.

You've probably used assessments in the past. For the most part, they are intended to point you to a quick fix or cookie-cutter solution. They often lack a biblical foundation and, at times, are loaded with the latest fads and principles. That's not the case here. Get ready for a different experience and result.

Finish this chapter, then take the Radical Alignment Assessment™ and begin your surprising journey by using this QR code or visiting our website.

ADVANCE

Your role is to advance, and keep advancing, with God's help and the Holy Spirit's guidance. Our role is to help.

Use the Radical Alignment Assessment™ to find out where you are and what to do next. Let the natural tension created by the gap between where you are, and where you want to be, inform your steps.

Alignment Aids. If you've tried to learn the game of golf, you've experienced the importance of alignment. In fact, alignment aids are a key segment of products in the golf market.

A coach can be pivotal in teaching you about alignment and how to achieve better swings. But a good coach will also teach you how to use alignment aids to force you into proper form so you can get reps without the coach always tagging along.

Sure, we offer coaching. It's a big part of our role in this movement. But ultimately, our tools are intended to be alignment aids by shaping the hearts, minds, and strength of everyone in your church, including you, so you can get the reps without us.

Remember, radical alignment can only occur when your motives, reasoning, and actions align to God's purposes.

We built the Intentional Churches Toolbox for this very purpose—to inspire and equip One-aware, activated, and radically aligned churches. It is designed to uniquely equip the Great Commission functions of your leadership team, board, and congregation.

The three-part toolbox is built to inspire, train, and equip your . . .

Team to lead a One-aware and activated church.

OneTeam

Board to shepherd a One-aware and activated church.

OneBoard

Congregation to live a One-aware and activated life.

OneLife

The Intentional Church Journey

As we've shared, the journey to becoming a One-aware, activated, and radically aligned church will take time and patience. It will involve the hearts, minds, and strength of everyone in your church, including you, in all its depth and dimensions.

The journey will not be identical, but will look similar for everyone involved. Here is a map that helps to illustrate it.

LEVEL 0	LEVEL 1	LEVEL 2	LEVEL 3	LEVEL 4	LEVEL 5
THE INTENTIONAL CHURCH JOURNEY						
Explore	Experience	Learn	Own	Live	Multiply

The Six Levels of the Intentional Church Journey

These levels and depths of adoption will look similar for everyone involved, personally and organizationally.

- **Level 0: Explore**
  Finding answers to questions like: who are you, where do I start, what do I do next, and how do I share this with my team?

- **Level 1: Experience**
  Exposure and engagement that leads to awareness and conviction.

- **Level 2: Learn**
  Understanding that leads to Holy Spirit–inspired action.

- **Level 3: Own**
  Deeper understanding of the Intentional Churches Toolbox and using it on a repeated basis as a leader or team.

- **Level 4: Live**
  Problem-solving and advancing without much help.

- **Level 5: Multiply**
  Helping others know what you know and experience it as well.

Deeper and Wider. Generally speaking, your role is to move deeper and wider, both personally and organizationally, into what it means to be radically aligned to the Great Commission.

Transformation of the Heart. Do your intentions, convictions, passions, and desires align with the mission of Jesus? *How about your leadership team? How about your congregation?*

Transformation of the Mind. Do you believe and understand the world as Jesus did? Do you think and reason as He did? *How about your leadership team? How about your congregation?*

Transformation of Strength. Do you process, pursue, and set priorities as Jesus did? Do you act as He acted? *How about your leadership team? How about your congregation?*

Here's How We Help

We've organized our ministry's resources in a way that can help you assess and advance on the Intentional Church journey.

Assessments
- Explore and engage
- Awareness that leads to conviction and action
- Answers: Where do I start, what do I do next?

Books, Studies, and the *Intentional Churches* Podcast
- Grow in knowledge personally and as a team
- Hear about the latest learning from the field

Training Engagements with a Coach (Laps)

- Install the Intentional Churches Toolbox with our help
- Live facilitation and training of your team
- Coaching from a trained church leader using the Intentional Churches Toolbox

Activator Training Events and Courses

- Experientially learn how to use each tool in the Intentional Churches Toolbox
- Join a community of like-minded and trained leaders

Intentional Churches Online Community

- Online hub for learning, installing, and using the Intentional Churches Toolbox
- Free resources and experiences for self-discovery and implementation
- Find leaders like you who are using the Intentional Churches Toolbox and approach

Intentional Churches Conference

- Annual live gathering for teams interested in using the Intentional Churches Toolbox and approach to ministry
- Always focused on radical alignment to the Great Commission
- Inspiration and training for every member of your team

Assess and Advance. By diligently assessing and taking steps to advance, you will be "installing" the Intentional Churches Toolbox as your personal and organizational operating system. We've found the journey to be very dynamic and not necessarily linear.

ABIDE

If you've let Scripture speak to you and didn't just take our word for it, you see this whole alignment thing differently now. We do, for sure.

One of the guiding beliefs at Intentional Churches is that we have little to do with growing or radically aligning our churches. The belief comes from Paul's words in 1 Corinthians 3:6, "I planted the seed in your hearts, and Apollos watered it, but it was God who made it grow."

If you are wearing new alignment lenses, you can see how this passage is closely linked to Jesus's words from John 15. A new way of living and leading requires a new (old) way of following.

> *You have already been pruned and purified by the message I have given you. Remain in me, and I will remain in you. For a branch cannot produce fruit if it is severed from the vine, and you cannot be fruitful unless you remain in me. Yes, I am the vine; you are the branches. Those who remain in me, and I in them, will produce much fruit. For apart from me you can do nothing.*
>
> —John 15:3–5

We recommend you pause and read John 15 right now. It's an incredible passage about radical alignment. It's a proof text for you and your team when it comes to personal alignment that naturally extends to your church.

We can sum it up like this: radical alignment with the Great Commission requires radical dependence on Christ.

Why is that important?

- He will empower His mission to "seek and save the lost" through you, doing immeasurably more than you can imagine. You become a conduit for the Good News with the Advocate of the Holy Spirit going before you.

- You are freed from the burden of the ultimate results. You have a job to do, but you can't produce the fruit. In fact, apart from Him, you can do nothing!

- You can be confident that as you are pruned, it's always on the way to bearing more fruit—fruit that lasts. You can make outrageous requests of the Father, and He will answer you. And all of this will bring Him glory.

Radical dependence doesn't make the journey easier, but it does make it possible. The only way to implement and radically align your church to the Great Commission is by first abiding in Christ.

The journey to becoming an Intentional Church really is a surprise. It's a surprise because it's a very personal invitation from the Almighty to partner in leading His Church. It's a surprise because it has been His purpose all along, and only through His power will it happen. Radical alignment is His to produce.

We leave you with our favorite Great Commission Scripture. It may be the most powerful call to personal radical alignment and the ultimate purpose for it. It's oozing with One-awareness and activation.

And all of this is a gift from God, who brought us back to himself through Christ. And God has given us this task of reconciling people to him. For God was in Christ, reconciling the world to himself, no longer counting people's sins against them. And he gave us this wonderful message of reconciliation. So we are Christ's ambassadors; God is making his appeal through us. We speak for Christ when we plead, "Come back to God!" For God made Christ, who never sinned, to be the offering for our sin, so that we could be made right with God through Christ.

—2 Corinthians 5:18–21

It's been an honor to share about the surprising journey of radical alignment and becoming an Intentional Church.

Let's do this together.

For Individual Reflection and Application:

1. Complete the Radical Alignment Assessment™. Based on your results, what are top growth areas? Create an action plan with steps for each area.

2. Reflect deeply on John 15:3-5. How does "abiding in Christ" practically affect your approach to church leadership and the Great Commission? How does this passage speak to alignment in your words?

3. What would it mean for you to live as Christ's ambassador, with God making his appeal through you (2 Corinthians 5:18-21)? What would need to change?

For Team Discussion and Interaction:

1. Review the six levels of the Intentional Church Journey (Explore, Experience, Learn, Own, Live, Multiply). Which level best describes where you are personally? What about your team? What is your next step?

2. Discuss as a team: Where should we start? How do we share this with others in our church and begin the journey together?

AN INTENTIONAL CHURCH STORY

From Brokenness to Great Commission Alignment: The Faith-filled Story of FC Newburgh

When disaster strikes and trust crumbles, can a church find its way back to radical alignment with the Great Commission? First Christian Church of Newburgh proves the answer is a resounding yes.

In 2005, an F3/F4 tornado devastated FC Newburgh's new building project, transforming a $6-8 million investment into a $13.5 million nightmare. The financial pressure fractured leadership, their founding pastor retired without succession planning and planted a competing church down the road, and their congregation plummeted from 1,400 to 700 in under a year. By 2021, they faced $9.9 million in debt with only 425 in weekly attendance. "We really should not be here," admitted Executive Director Holly Gillespie.

The Turning Point

Rather than pursuing another quick fix, FC Newburgh partnered with Intentional Churches, discovering that sustainable transformation required long-term strategy, not silver bullets. "When you have that evaluation piece, you're no longer striving for a fix, you're striving for progress," explains Teaching Pastor Nathan Logsdon. The Intentional Church Model didn't try to force them into a mold—instead, it drew out their unique calling while providing the cohesive language and radical alignment they desperately needed.

Radical Alignment in Action

Today, FC Newburgh exemplifies what happens when a church gets radically aligned to the Great Commission. Their leadership team operates with unified vision, their congregation responds strategically rather than reactively, and their ministry has transformed from survival mode to multiplication focus. Their heartbeat now centers on "Ones reaching Ones"—building authentic relationships that invite others into life together.

The Redemption Reality

Lead Pastor Kevin Brimner reflects, "From fall of 2021 to today, we have learned to own our story, not as one of failure, but one of redemption." Their journey proves that even churches facing seemingly impossible circumstances can find their way back to health and Great Commission effectiveness through intentional alignment, patient process, and refusing to abandon God's calling on their lives.

For pastors wondering if breakthrough is possible, FC Newburgh's story offers hope: radical alignment to the Great Commission isn't just possible after crisis—it might be the very thing that transforms your greatest challenges into your most powerful testimony.

Read FC Newburgh's Full Story Here

FOUNDATIONS

25 Foundational Beliefs

These statements form the foundations of our coaching, training, and equipping of One-aware, activated, and radically aligned churches. We hope and pray they become the guiding beliefs of every Intentional Church.

Mission and Vision Foundations

WE BELIEVE the Great Commission is the mission. We don't believe you need months to craft a clever mission statement when Jesus already gave the church one in Matthew 28:19–20: "Go and make disciples." Furthermore, we believe it's not only an organizational mission, it's a personal mission given to every believer. The mission never changes but methods and strategies to accomplish it will, over time.

WE BELIEVE vision must stretch churches and leaders. We champion the "double impact in five years or less" framework because it is clear and helpful. We help leaders embrace the healthy tension that robust vision creates because it sparks innovative thinking and courageous decision-making. We also think it honors God. We partner with churches to set ambitious visions where faith is tested and the work ahead becomes clear.

WE BELIEVE future vision should be renewed on a regular basis because God's plans are always evolving. Mission is static but vision is dynamic and must be held loosely, and refreshed regularly. We guide leaders to plan vision renewal every one to two years because God often does immeasurably more than we hope or imagine when we align with His mission. We work with churches to stay nimble and responsive to what God is doing in each new season rather than clinging to yesterday's plans.

WE BELIEVE every church is a unique creation by God. We challenge leaders to not copy other churches' visions and strategies, and instead discover how God wants to accomplish the Great

Commission through their church. These outcomes can be very unique between churches, even if two churches sit next door to one another. Churches are not competing with on another when it comes to the Great Commission.

WE BELIEVE the mission and clear vision create a "true north" from which to measure success. "Is the mission being accomplished?" and "Is the vision unfolding?" are the only pertinent questions. We push leaders to judge progress apart from personal preferences, feelings, or traditional church metrics. We challenge churches to ruthlessly eliminate activities that don't advance their mission and vision, no matter how comfortable or traditional they may be.

WE BELIEVE unity in leadership is a great weapon against Satan's schemes. Leaders must remain radically unified around mission, vision, and strategy. We facilitate healthy, objective conversations about the future while refusing to give into personal agendas and destructive undercurrents. We seek to build leadership cultures that are so unified the enemy finds no foothold for division.

Church Growth and Strategy Foundations

WE BELIEVE church growth is God's design and expectation. The Church was created to grow and leaders must be concerned about the depth and breadth of its impact. More and better disciples will create more and better impact. We push pastors to expect, plan for, and work toward consistent growth while knowing that, ultimately, it's God's job to grow the church. We help churches determine healthy ways to measure and monitor their growth and kingdom impact. All measuring and monitoring, while emotional at times, is a part of the process in discerning God's direction.

WE BELIEVE best practices exist and champion proven practices while rejecting one-size-fits-all solutions. We develop leaders who are lifelong learners, adapting ministry practices to their unique context and calling. We provide fundamentals and tools based on biblical principles that allow continuous evaluation, learning, and strategic improvement. Our tools help to "test and approve" what is right instead of relying on a blind hunt for the next solution.

WE BELIEVE your "Jerusalem or Antioch" are very important when it comes to the Great Commission. Global impact flows from effective local ministry. We guide churches to prioritize Great Commission activation in their immediate community and see global missions as the outflow of making more and better disciples at home base. We develop leaders who become stewards of both local effectiveness and global ripple effects.

WE BELIEVE the gospel contains ALL the power to transform lives and communities. Transformation power lives in the gospel message, not human effort or clever strategies. We remind leaders to plant and water faithfully while trusting God for supernatural increase. We help churches discern their seasonal assignments and execute them with both excellence and complete dependence on God's power.

WE BELIEVE in seeking balance to Great Commission execution and outcomes—more AND better disciples. Churches must pursue balance in attractional, communal, and missional strategies while focusing on those yet to be reached. In Acts, we see an attractive church, rich community, and a church mobilized and in action. We believe all of those aspects of the church are important while revolving around an undeniable focus and bias toward reaching the lost. A church will likely never achieve perfect balance but it must fight for strategic equilibrium as it seeks to imitate the strategies of the early church.

WE BELIEVE prayer and the Holy Spirit fuel the mission. Human strategies without divine power will accomplish little if anything that is lasting. We insist churches pray first, then plan and execute with complete dependence on the Holy Spirit's wisdom and guidance. We help leaders create prayer cultures that undergird every Great Commission initiative.

Evangelism and Discipleship Foundations

WE BELIEVE everything must be biased toward "The One" in order to achieve balanced Great Commission outcomes. Churches must shape strategies, vision, and execution toward reaching those who do not know Jesus as Savior. It might be counterintuitive, but this focus helps a church maintain a balance of more and better disciples. We challenge leaders to constantly fight the natural church drift toward inward focus and member preferences. We help pastors keep lost people at the center of every decision, every dollar, and every ministry initiative.

WE BELIEVE grace creates the environment where truth can transform lives. Churches must lead with grace while remaining anchored in biblical truth. We guide leaders to create environments where lost people belong before they believe, knowing that grace-filled spaces produce the deepest life change. We help churches emphasize grace without compromising truth.

WE BELIEVE evangelistic focus is a great way to create deep disciples. Focusing on lost people produces incredibly committed and mature followers of Jesus because a follower must realize the church is not there to serve his or her needs alone. Followers are challenged to become more selfless in a "One-aware and activated" church. We help leaders show followers that the Church exists to be on Jesus' mission of seeking and saving the lost.

WE BELIEVE evangelistic potential is exponentially larger than churches imagine. Every church's relational reach extends far beyond weekend attendance to hundreds, thousands, or even tens of thousands of relational connections. We help leaders envision and expand their church's evangelistic impact through these relationships by equipping every believer to live a "One-aware and activated" life. Even a small ministry or church plant has tremendous potential to reach the lost through relationships.

WE BELIEVE conversion growth is growth that matters. Churches must plan for growth primarily through reaching people who do not yet know Jesus as Savior and Lord. We challenge leaders to prioritize conversion growth versus shuffling believers between congregations. We also challenge leaders to eliminate erroneous thoughts of church competition because of proximity or unfounded concepts of cultural saturation.

WE BELIEVE discipleship happens through fundamental activities that never change. While every discipleship pathway is unique, the fundamentals remain constant across cultures and generations. We guide leaders to engage people in gathering for worship and preaching, life-changing relationships, and increasing surrender through sacrifice and service—the biblical strategies of the early church. We help churches partner with God in individual transformation through these proven, biblical pathways.

Stewardship and Resources Foundations

WE BELIEVE leaders are temporary stewards of God's eternal church, and responsible to pass it to the next generation in optimal condition. We challenge pastors to lead with the urgency of those who must give account for their stewardship. We help churches make decisions from a stewardship mindset rather than an ownership mentality. The Church is forever the bride and body of Christ, but it's only temporarily in our hands.

WE BELIEVE attention is sacred currency. Attention has become a precious commodity in our distracted world. We challenge leaders to treat every moment of captured focus as sacred ground for pointing people toward Jesus and leading a "One-aware and activated" church. We help churches use the four commodities of life and leadership—time, money, energy, and attention—with laser focus to lead His Church and advance the Great Commission.

WE BELIEVE every resource matters and every leadership decision is zero-sum—there is no innocent "yes." Every dollar and minute spent in one area cannot be spent elsewhere. We push leaders to make strategic trade-offs that maximize Great Commission impact. We help churches evaluate every opportunity, program, and initiative through the lens of "One-awareness and activation." Every square foot, dollar, and minute matters for eternal impact. We help churches use their God-given resources with the intensity of stewards who know there will be an account and that eternity hangs in the balance.

Coaching and Training Foundations

WE BELIEVE self-discovery is far more powerful than consulting. Self-discovery creates lasting transformation while consulting creates temporary dependence. We begin with honest, team-based conversations and assessments, not consultant-based evaluations. When we start our work with our opinions and insights, we sometimes create distraction, division, and discouragement rather than breakthrough, ownership, and clarity. We believe deeply that team-based, Socratic, reflective tools and processes help build resilient plans to accomplish the Great Commission.

WE BELIEVE churches are better together, collaborating rather than competing. Church leaders must collaborate and learn from one another from the trenches of ministry. No single local church can accomplish God's mission in the world alone. Every gospel-centered church should have a plan to take spiritual ground in the name of His mission. We must collaboratively link arms to make this happen at a world-changing scale.

WE BELIEVE the goal of every engagement and resource is to foster independence, not dependence. Our aim is to equip others in a way that does not create dependence on us. Thus, we provide tools, training, and resources for churches to operate without us. Our aim is to see churches adopt our model, the Intentional Churches Toolbox, as their operating system for the purposes of collaboration and synergy. We seek to activate the Great Commission in as many churches as possible, leading to increasing impact generation after generation.

WE BELIEVE we are stewards of this growing movement, but not the only ones. It's in the hands of any and every Intentional Church. To God be the glory!

About the Authors

Bart Rendel, Intentional Churches cofounder: Bart's passion for serving churches comes from his upbringing as a pastor's kid and learning from his parents about the intentionality of reaching and growing people in Christ. His conviction runs deep. Bart served as an executive leader for over eighteen years at Crossroads Christian Church in Lexington, Kentucky, and Central Christian Church in Las Vegas, Nevada, where he remains deeply connected. He and his wife, Catherine, have two children.

Doug Parks, Intentional Churches cofounder: Doug's love and commitment to helping churches comes from his own experience of being eternally impacted as a teenager by a committed church leader. He served for seventeen years as the executive pastor at Canyon Ridge Christian Church in Las Vegas, Nevada. Prior to ministry, Doug was a Symbol of Success award-winning owner/operator at Chick-fil-A. Doug and his wife, Jennifer, have two children and reside in Las Vegas, Nevada.